The Hard-Core Speak

by

Elsa Curyk

Note for Librarians: a cataloguing record for this book that includes Dewey Decimal Classification and US Library of Congress numbers is available from the Library and Archives of Canada. The complete cataloguing record can be obtained from their online database at:

www.collectionscanada.ca/amicus/index-e.html

ISBN 1-4120-4669-6

Printed in Victoria, BC, Canada

TRAFFORD

Offices in Canada, USA, Ireland, UK and Spain

This book was published *on-demand* in cooperation with Trafford Publishing. On-demand publishing is a unique process and service of making a book available for retail sale to the public taking advantage of on-demand manufacturing and Internet marketing. On-demand publishing includes promotions, retail sales, manufacturing, order fulfilment, accounting and collecting royalties on behalf of the author.

Book sales for North America and international:

Trafford Publishing, 6E–2333 Government St.,

Victoria, BC v8t 4p4 CANADA

phone 250 383 6864 (toll-free 1 888 232 4444)

fax 250 383 6804; email to orders@trafford.com

Book sales in Europe:

Trafford Publishing (uk) Ltd., Enterprise House, Wistaston Road Business Centre,

Wistaston Road, Crewe, Cheshire cw2 7rp UNITED KINGDOM

phone 01270 251 396 (local rate 0845 230 9601)

facsimile 01270 254 983; orders.uk@trafford.com

Order online at:

www.trafford.com/robots/04-2477.html

10 9 8 7 6 5 4 3

Table of Contents

Foreword

This is a true story. It must be told for the sake of all the young people with whom I have served as an English teacher.

For the past ten years I have worked with the "hard-core" street gang members of East and South Central Los Angeles. During that time I have collected their poetry, essays, and auto-biographies, through which the "hard-core" reveal their hearts and their minds. I have had the unique opportunity to work in a federally funded criminal justice diversion project, as well as in a special "barrio" school for gang members.

Through this teaching experience I have gained insight into why some young people join gangs and how they feel about themselves as gang members. This special insight could lead to more successful and realistic programs for rehabilitation wherein public money would not be spent on self-defeating programs.

THE HARD-CORE SPEAK is about some of the pitfalls that could be avoided if we were really serious about saving our inner-city youth.

But Is Anyone Listening?

Chapter One

THE BARRIO SCHOOL

The "Barrio School" came into existence through the continued efforts of the Chicano Affirmative Action programs.

Organized demonstrations and sit-ins had produced some fruit. Emilio Rosas had emerged as the most trusted community leader in the seventies. As an adult school teacher at an East Los Angeles Skills Center, he had come in contact with many street gang youth who were not in school and had no jobs nor much hope for a better future. Most hung around local parks, drinking and getting high. After talking to them and their parents, Rosas realized that most of them were actually afraid to go to school for fear of reprisals from rival gangs.

The gang with whom Rosas mainly worked called themselves the "Mariposa," named after a street on which most of them lived. Their turf included only several blocks, yet in this small territory eight gang-related murders and many drug overdosed had occurred within a one-year period. Unemployment, alcoholism, hopelessness, and a general decay were the predominant spirit of this barrio.

Parents were desperate for a better way of life for their children. They turned to the local Catholic Church for support and for answers. A young clergyman, Brother Modesto, became the champion of these lost young people. His idea was to organize a school just for them where they could continue their education without fear of harassment.

Emilio Rosas aligned himself with Brother Modesto. Together they held community meetings and persuaded the parents to organize themselves, go before the board of education, and demand equal education for their sons and daughters. A large percentage of the students had been expelled, suspended, or dropped out. Those who remained in school were often functionally illiterate. Rosas was convinced of the Anglo school system's inability to effectively understand or deal with the special needs of the barrio youth.

School officials met with community leaders, parents, and the local church. Brother Ernesto, the spokesperson for the group, was there to inform school representatives of the special needs of the community. The Los Angels schools agreed to cooperate with the community, school records were checked, and it was established that about thirty high school students in the barrio could not attend the local high school.

After many meetings and compromises a decision was reached to establish a continuation-education school with two teachers of the required subjects. The school would also provide a part-time school clerk. The Catholic Church contributed two brothers to work full-time as teacher's aides.

The newly formed P.T.A. promised that at least two mothers would always be on hand to help with discipline. We teachers were just to teach. The clergy and the mothers would handle the discipline, because it was a known fact that Chicano youth had a deep respect for religion and motherhood, though fleetingly the thought occurred to me to wonder why they led such a destructive lifestyle if they had so much respect for mother and priest.

Dr. Blake, my administrator, approached me with an offer to teach in the new East Los Angeles Continuation School. He explained that the student body now consisted mainly of young people who had been out of school for quite a while because of fear of gang activity. For fear of their safety, their parents would now allow them to attend regular school. I naturally assumed that these would be quiet and shy students who were deprived of an education because of a hostile, threatening environment.

Dr. Blake told me that this would be an experimental program, a community-based school with strong parental involvement as well as support from the local Catholic Church. In fact, two priests volunteered to be full-time tutors until the students caught up with their basic skills. He also informed me that two mothers would be in the classroom at all times, helping with supervision and discipline. In my naivete I thought this was an ideal arrangement, since dealing with discipline was not one of my favorite tasks, although I did wonder why these shy, quiet kids needed so much supervision.

Dr. Blake informed me that he selected me for this special task because he believed that I would work well with Emilio Rosas, the other teacher in the new program. Dr. Blake told me that the board of education had to give Rosas an emergency credential to teach high school subjects, since he was an adult school teacher, but the community had specifically requested him as the teacher of their children because of the special relationship he had established with so many of the boys.

We initially would begin with twenty students each and gradually increase the enrollment. We would use a bungalow with two classrooms and a kitchen. These facilities belonged to adult education, but they agreed to share them with us during the day.

The next morning I was to meet with the other team member, Emilio Rosas, at our new location in order to become acquainted and to discuss our program, division of responsibilities, teaching strategies, and general goals for the year. We knew this was an experimental program and many people would be watching us.

I liked Emilio immediately. He was energetic, positive, and attractive. He would teach the math and science classes, while I would teach English, social studies, and American History. Emilio had already decorated his classroom with poster of Emiliano Zapata, Pancho Villa, and other modern revolutionaries with their clenched-fist salute.

We heard a knock on the door.

Rosas went to open it. "Oh, come in, Joe."

"I just came to check on the progress of your school."

"Joe, I want you to meet Elsa."

"Hi, Elsa. Aren't you a Chicana? You look like one. You must be married to an Anglo."

Before I had a chance to answer, Emilio interrupted. "Elsa, this is Joe Vargas. He's the principal of the adult school. He's kind enough to let us use his facilities for the Barrio School."

I extended my hand to Joe for a handshake. "No, Joe, I'm not a Chicana, but people have told me that I look Mexican or Spanish. Actually, I'm German and Polish, but to me nationality isn't important. It's personality that counts."

After the usual courtesies, Joe turned to Emilio.

With passion in his eyes and voice, he proclaimed, "Listen, Rosas, I know your political views, and you know I don't share them. Those posters will have to come off the walls. This is my building. Adult school is a conservative institution. We don't agree with flaming revolutionaries. We believe in hard work and good education as a way of raising oneself out of these slums. Education gives us opportunities, not your leftist bullshit. The students we serve here at night don't want to come around here and look at this leftist propaganda. Many of them had to leave their countries because of the 'revolution.'"

With rage in his eyes, Rosas replied, "What kind of a Chicano are you? You've become a real Oreo. You're siding with the oppressor against your own people."

"You're blind, Ross!" Joe yelled back. "The gang kids you'll be teaching don't need any enticement to revolution. They're already antisocial and destructive enough. They haven't been oppressed. They're just goddamned lazy, fucked-up kids who would rather steal and get drunk than do an honest day's work. It's their parents' fault. Their parents are mostly drunks, jailbirds, and welfare recipients. They haven't been taught any respect at home, so they have none for society.

"You'll find out soon enough, Rosas, like I did. Then we'll have another more informed talk. You'll see. These kids don't need revolution. They need evolution. They need to evolve from their narrow little animal minds to thinking, caring human minds. You're not gonna do it with your revolutionary bullshit. Teach them to create, not to destroy! I want those posters off by tomorrow, or none of you will be here! The taxpayers are not going to support revolutionaries with their hard-earned money, understand?

Joe slammed the door as he left in a cloud of disgust.

Emilio turned to me. "See what we'll be up against? We can't expect much support from the establishment. Joe is just a typical middle-class reactionary who thinks only of his own narrow self-interest. That's why progress is so slow in society. Most people can't see farther than their stomachs. We'll play the game for a while so not to jeopardize the program. I know Joe. I've already anticipated his reaction. It's important to remain calm and go about our business."

He removed most of the militant posters. Just a couple with Viva la Raza remained.

His last comment upon the whole matter was, "Above all else, one must collaborate with the enemy until he is destroyed. Let's get to work, Elsa. We've wasted too much time already, listening to that bigot."

We drove to the board of education to pick up our school books for all the subjects we would be teaching. We loaded up our cars with books, materials, and new supplies.

It was exciting to get a new program, because there was so much optimism, so much expectation. We had a chance to remedy all the educational blunders that had been perpetrated against these innocent children. We would motivate them to learn, to raise their consciousness. They would become inspired to go to college or learn a valuable trade. We headed back in high spirits, ready to organize our rooms, the conflict of a couple of hours earlier all but forgotten.

My classroom-to-be was large, with plenty of tables and chairs. We wanted to stay away from the traditional desks arranged neatly in rows like pews. This was not to be a traditional classroom environment, the kind that turned them off in the first place. No traditional stifling regimentation would creep into this room. Students were to feel free and welcome in the style of Summerhill. We would encourage but not force. We would motivate but not threaten.

All children naturally want to learn if given the proper nurturing environment. Our educational philosophies coincided perfectly. The child was never wrong. Only the system or the method was wrong if the child did not succeed. Both of us were most anxious to try our humane and humanistic methods.

Emilio knocked on my door, telling me that the two student priests had arrived and wanted to meet both of us before we started working with the students. Emilio introduced me to both of them.

Brother John was a short, balding young man with watery blue eyes and low vitality. He appeared to be of Irish descent. Brother Fernando, however, was the exact opposite – tall, slender, obviously of Latin descent. He had thick, curly black hair and perfect features. His penetrating green eyes reminded me of pictures of the ancient mystics.

<u>Why does he want to be a priest</u>? I wondered, <u>What pain is he hiding from? He could be a great actor</u>.

His black habit reminded me, however, that this was no ordinary man but someone more elevated, a man of God. Still, there has to be human conflict to drive a man to seek refuge in the priesthood. The "Barrio School" definitely would be an experience!

Just as the two student priests were leaving, two of the volunteer mothers arrived. Rosas introduced them as Mrs. Chavez and Mrs. Estrada, both attractive women in their early forties. They seemed pleased by the way we had arranged our classrooms, and both expressed their hopes for a successful venture. I liked both women, and we soon dropped the formalities.

"All this 'Mrs. Chavez' and 'Mrs. Estrada' makes us feel so old and dignified, Mrs. Chavez said. "I'm Rita, and this is Connie. Each of us has a couple of children in this program. We'll be here every day to help out."

"My name is Elsa," I responded, "and I don't believe in all the formality either. It just puts distance between people, and we already have too much distance between people. That's why we can't get along."

"We're happy to have you with us, Elsa. Doctor Blake made a good decision when he sent you."

"Thank you, Connie and Rita. I'm looking forward to working with all of you."

"Tomorrow we'll send you around twenty students who have already pre-registered with Brother Ernesto," Connie informed me. "You know he is getting quite a name for himself nationally, working with these gang kids. The kids are anxious to come to their own school. They know we fought real hard to get it."

Rosas told the mothers to have the students here promptly at eight o'clock or a little before. We would be dividing them into two groups. The math and science groups would be with Rosas, and the English and history groups would be with me. Each class would last two hours, after which we would have a twenty-minute nutrition break. Then the students would switch classes for another two hours of study. They would have a free lunch, provided by the board of education, and by one p.m. the students were dismissed. Rosas had to hurry to his second job at the skills center to teach adult classes.

Both mothers were pleased by the proposed schedule, telling us that some of their sons and daughters had been out of school for two years and that they would have a hard time becoming accustomed to getting up early in the morning. Rita and Connie promised to call all the mothers to inform them that classes would begin tomorrow and what the schedule would be.

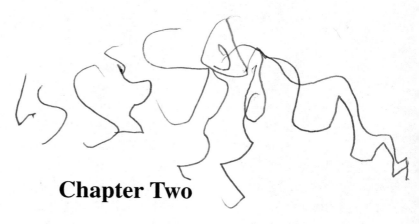

Chapter Two

THE FIRST DAY

Rosas and I arrived early to prepare ourselves to register and pretest our new arrivals. We wanted to know their reading levels and their math skills.

This was to be an individualized program, tailored to each student's need. There were to be no class lectures nor class discussion. Students were not to compete with each other for grades. They were to compete only with themselves, each day growing in their assigned classwork. We were anxious to help these students who were so long deprived of an education.

Shortly after eight o'clock they began arriving in small groups. The boys, with their neatly clipped hair slicked back, immaculately white t-shirts, and creased pants, looked as though they were pressed from the same mold. How could I ever tell them apart? They all looked alike to me. There was no individuality. They all appeared to represent some stereotype of each other, even to the neatly folded bandanas tucked into their back pockets.

The girls all wore heavy white face makeup with thick black eyeliner and rows of long false eyelashes. Their hair was heavily teased in the sixties style. All the girls wore creased corduroys.

So these are the children who are afraid to go to school.

I began to get the picture. The principal was not exactly lying when he said that these students were afraid to attend school. He just omitted a minor detail – the reason that they were afraid.

Shortly Rita and Connie arrived with more students. I had them sit in a group around a large table, passing out paper and pencils. I introduced myself as their new teacher and explained how this class would be different from the ones they had been used to.

I explained the individualized program to them. They would each have two folders in each class with the lessons outlined for the whole semester. When one of them completed the contract, he would receive five credits per course toward his high-school diploma. It would be up to him how fast he wanted to work. A really motivated student could make up his credits fast and return to regular school if he so desired, or he could graduate from continuation school.

Before assigning them any books, I wanted to know their reading levels and their English skills. I asked each one to write a short autobiography stating the schools that he had attended, his family situation, his interests, and above all, what he expected from this program now that they had a school of their own. I explained that as they wrote, I would call them up individually for a short oral reading test.

I looked at the faces with their blank expressions. Did they understand me?

"Do you understand the assignment, class?" I asked in my most professional voice.

There were still more blank stares.

I walked over to Connie and asked, "Do they speak English?"

"Of course!" was Connie's surprised reply. "They were born here."

A tall, chubby girl raised her hand. "Miss, what did you say to write? Bio...? A biology?"

"Oh, I'd better explain in more detail. Who knows what an autobiography is?"

More blank stares followed.

I went on to explain what an autobiography is, reassuring them that I was not prying into their life, merely trying to determine their level of English and reading skills in order to give them the proper assignments and not to waste so much time before determining if certain books were too easy or too hard for them. This explanation seemed to make more sense to most of them. Some settled down to write as I called them, one by one, to my desk for the reading placement test.

I was shocked by their lack of reading skills. Most were on the third- or fourth-grade level. Some were even as low as the second-grade level. Some had to be prompted continuously. My beautiful new tenth- and eleventh-grade literature anthologies were definitely inappropriate. Where could I get some elementary school materials?

I walked around the room to see how they were doing with their writing assignment. To my disbelief, most were practicing their graffiti writing skills, which were quite impressive. Some really were good artists, and I complimented them on their artistic skills.

They smiled and looked at me with surprise, <u>What kind of teacher is this, actually enjoying graffiti?</u>

The immensity of the task finally dawned on me. Did Doctor Blake know about the problems we would be facing here? Why did he choose me, a real innocent, an idealist? Did he think that lack of knowledge, total naivete were qualities that made for success of this program?

At that time I had no idea that this whole experiment was based on political power play. Rosas and I were merely the sacrificial lambs of the power brokers; yet Rosas and I came without any preconceived notions about those students. We had no opinions about their lack of motivation or their intellectual ability. We did not stereotype them in any way. Perhaps we did have a better chance to reach them than someone with more sophistication.

More students started to arrive. It was an hour after class was supposed to begin. Rita apologized for the tardies, saying that she called most of the mothers to remind them that finally their own school would be in session. She promised that tomorrow she would personally give many students "wake-up calls."

Finally the school day ended. I could not wait to compare notes with Rosas.

I hurried into his classroom, asking, "How did it go?"

He replied, "You won't believe this, but most of the kids don't know their multiplication tables. They don't know the most elementary principles of arithmetic. They tell me that they forgot! Some of them haven't been to school for three years. I believe they couldn't even read the instructions to the most simple math problems."

"I believe you, Emilio. All morning long I've tried to get them to write autobiographies. Now that was a joke. They looked at me as if I were from outer space. The oral reading test was a real eye-opener. I used the Grey Oral Reading Test. It's pretty superficial, but you get an immediate idea where a student is. I couldn't believe it either. Most of them read on the third- and fourth-grade level. Some appear to have only second-grade reading skills."

Emilio's angry reply was, "That just goes to show you how inadequate and prejudiced the Anglo school system is. Did you know that many of the Mexican kids who come here were put into classes for the mentally retarded? Yes, the E.M.R. classes – emotionally and mentally constipated. Now we see the result of this mental constipation. They are just continuing the welfare and the poverty level of the browns and the blacks. They kick them out or push them out, but they call them 'dropouts.' Did you know that most of the principals come from the physical education department? They are all a bunch of militaristic hard-asses. Any intellectual or enlightened thought freezes in their icy brains – and we, the taxpayers, pay their fat salaries to fuck up our kids, to make them feel like imbeciles, like criminals."

Rosas finished his speech, really angry.

"I see what you mean," was my surprised reply. "What are we going to do with all those anthologies and history books?"

"We'll keep them! You'll see, those kids will improve fast with all this individual help."

"Good idea, Rosas! I think I'll go back to Doctor Blake's office and tell him about what we've discovered here today. I'm sure he has some easier materials for us. At this point I wish I were an elementary school teacher, because I don't know anything about teaching reading, but I'd better learn fast."

"You'll do fine, Elsa. The kids told me they like you. They said you were 'cool' and 'funny.' Chin up!"

Rosas' remarks helped to cheer me up a bit.

Doctor Blake had that knowing grin on his face when I told him about my experience that morning. "Of course, Elsa, we have high-interest, low-reading-level books. Just help yourself to anything there is in the storeroom. For teaching elementary reading, a lot of teachers have had good success with the Doctor Spello books. It deals mainly with the phonetic approach to reading. Take one home and go over it. You'll find out something about teaching. We come to teach, but we end up learning much more. You'll see, all of us – the community leaders, the mothers, priests, you, me, Rosas – all will learn much from this program. I'll warn you right now. We might not particularly like what we will learn. It may not fit in with our preconceived notions about reality. As the song goes, 'We lose our starry notions, one by one.'"

"Doctor Blake, I'm wondering why you chose me for this project. I've been teaching for only a couple of years in a well-established, structured program."

"And I've heard find reports about you from the director – but I chose you because you have certain life experience. You have gone through the Second World War. You lost your father in the concentration camps. You're raising three children alone. So you have no illusions about human nature, yet you have a certain compassion toward people. The rest you'll learn fast, a sort of on-the-job training. My advice to you is, work on their self-images! All studies so far show that kids with a gang mentality suffer from a very low self-image. They are afraid and insecure when alone, but together in a group they feel powerful. Studies also show that these kids have a low frustration tolerance and a short attention span. Learning and concentration are actually anxiety-producing experiences for them, so devise lessons to decrease or remove their anxiety stemming from past failures. Some of the hot-headed community leaders love to blame everything on the rotten school system. They'll have something to learn from this, and then they'll shut up."

"Thank you, Doctor Blake, for your invaluable advice. Yes, I'll keep working on their self-image. How do you do that, by the way?" I asked eagerly.

"Now that's a good question, Elsa. Nobody seems to know. Each individual is different. What works for one might not work for another. Just keep trying, and stay flexible."

"Will do!" was my cheery reply.

Being a teacher is like being a mother, I thought. With some kids you are a great parent, but with others you're not so great – a real mystery.

On the whole, I felt quite encouraged by Doctor Blake. He was a man of experience in the educational field. He knew how to get along with people, a real diplomat. He could work with any agency or any faction. He knew how to get the best from people. He had mastered the art of compromise. His insight into human character and motivation made him an effective administrator. No wonder he went far "up the hill."

With the new, easier books and Doctor Blake's encouragement, I was ready for another eventful day. New students arrived, all pressed from the same mold. How could I ever memorize their names? This was no easy job. They called each other – eh ese – El Chinito, La Loca, La Wina, El Payaso, etc. At that time I had absolutely no knowledge of Spanish or the gang culture. Innocently I asked one of the mothers, Rita, whether I should call the students by their Spanish name or American names.

She looked at me, puzzled. "They are Americans. They were born here. Naturally you call them by their first names, which are usually American."

"But they call each other different names from those I have in the roll book. I thought El Chinito or La Wina was Spanish, isn't it?"

"Oh, those names. Those are their gang names. When you join, you are given a very personal name according to your characteristics. If you smile a lot, you may be called La Smiley, or if your skin is dark, you might be called El Negro.

"I see," was my ignorant reply. "What about <u>La Wina</u>. Why do they call her that name?

"Because she drinks more wine than any of them. See her size?"

"How much does she weigh?"

"I'd say over two hundred pounds," Rita replied. "Only people in the 'in crowd' call each other those names. We adults call them by their proper names."

So, Doctor Blake was right again. I was learning much more than I was teaching.

After testing all the students, I distributed new manila folders to them with their contract or lesson plans stapled to one side. I asked the students to write their names on the folders that were used in the school records, because when they finished each contract, be it English 10A or 10B, American literature, or social studies, they would receive five high-school credits toward graduation requirements. Then they could decorate their folders in any way they pleased, as long as it was in good taste and would not offend any adults. They agreed that it was important to use their legal names in order to receive the proper credits.

The students really liked this assignment. They got busy right away decorating their folders with graffiti and their <u>placas</u>. Those who had talent started drawing low-rider cars and beautiful <u>cholas</u> perched on them.

They were all busily decorating their folders as I became more anxious and frustrated. Finally I had to explain to them that they were here to earn their credits as fast as possible, and to graduate. This was not an art school and I was unfortunately not an art teacher, although a lot of them had plenty of talent. I encouraged some of them to major in art when they got back to regular high school. With a lot of prodding, finally some of them did begin their work.

When the nutrition break came, some students started taking longer and longer breaks. Rosas had to constantly lecture the guys on their responsibility to the reputation of the school, and often reminded them of the privilege of having their own school. Some had been reported to sneak to the park to take a few gulps of wine.

One day during the break, a policeman came to the school office with two students in tow. He said that they had been drinking in the park. Then he began looking around the office, lifting the couch and armchair cushions. He said that he was looking for weapons, and to our surprise, he produced a couple of pocket knives that were hidden under the cushions.

Rosas stood there becoming red with rage, but he controlled himself. He knew direct confrontation with the police was totally unproductive. The boys, more and more, now looked to Rosas as a father figure. They respected him.

As the policeman was leaving, he looked at the assembled boys and said, "So you think you're tough? Well, we're the toughest gang in East L.A. You're just a bunch of boys who don't know how to be men yet."

Now Rosas turned his anger on the boys. He called the class together, telling them that attending this school was a privilege. It could be closed soon if they persisted in this type of behavior. He told them that there were people out there just waiting for incidents such as today to close the school.

He said some neighbors were afraid to see them all assembled in one place. They believe that a rival gang might see them as sitting ducks, and they might engage in gang warfare. The neighbors feared that their children might be caught in the crossfire of bullets, since the elementary school was nearby. The boys hung their heads like naughty children and promised never to do this again. They promised to respect their school.

The two student priests were coming every day to help with the tutoring. Most of the girls liked their attention and asked for help. The boys, however, were more reticent.

Eventually we all settled into a comfortable routine. Uppermost in my mind remained Doctor Blake's advice to improve the students' self-image to where they felt self-motivated. Then I would have achieved my primary purpose of being an educator.

Frankly, I felt quite ill-prepared for this new challenge. Even Brother Fernando said that they needed more "professional" personnel to be more effective with these students. I agreed with him. I told him that I did not consider myself an expert on teaching gang youth and asked him whether he knew any "experts." He admitted that he knew none of these, but there must be some around somewhere.

"Don't worry, Brother Fernando. If we stick with this long enough, we'll be the 'experts.'"

"God grant me the patience," was his only reply.

This feeling of inadequacy inspired me to enroll at U.C.L.A. in their reading specialist program. In a couple of years I would have a master's degree in education, plus be a reading specialist. Then perhaps I would be more successful in reaching these students.

I remember being really impressed by Dr. Louise L. Taylor's article in The Journal of Educational Research, "The Concept of an Ideal Teacher-Student Relationship." There she listed four essential criteria that promote learning:

1. The teacher give and takes in the classroom situation.
2. The teacher sees the student as a coworker on a common problem.

3. The teacher is sympathetic about the student's problems.
4. The teacher is well able to understand the student's ideas.

I was determined to apply these principles in my relationship with my students. As we became more acquainted, we developed mutual trust and friendship.

I felt that Rita and Connie were two good friends of mine. There was no tension between us. They supported me in all ways they possibly could. My relationship with the students became more relaxed and open. We began communicating on an individual human-to-human basis, not primarily teacher-to-student.

As students were released from juvenile hall, they enrolled in the Barrio School. We always had new students coming in. The older ones had settled down to work, but the new ones always posed new challenges. They had not been accustomed to the routine of regular school work and the discipline of concentration.

One boy, Mousy, took a particularly long time to settle down to work. Neither the mothers nor the priests could encourage him. He seemed very unhappy and not as well groomed as the rest of the students.

One day I asked him whether he wanted to go to the bank with me after school, and then we could stop and have a hamburger at Macdonald's. He liked that idea. During lunch I asked him why he was so nervous and could not concentrate on work, why he was always trying to disturb the rest of the class.

"I'm sorry, miss, but I have many problems," he said. "I haven't been learning anything for four years. I don't have a mother anymore, and my father is in prison for life, but if he ever should get out, my brother and I are going to kill him."

"That's a terrible thing to say, Mousy."

"No, it's not. See, four years ago he killed my mother right in our front yard. She was so beautiful, and he was always jealous of her. He called her all kinds of ugly names. They were all lies. She loved all of us so much. She stayed home and took good care of us. Then that bastard killed her like she was some mean dog."

"Oh, my God!" I cried with tears streaming down my face. "Where were you at the time?"

"All four of us kids were in the house. We heard the argument and then the shots. We ran out and started crying and screaming. Our father kept saying, 'I'm sorry, I'm sorry. She made me do it.' The neighbor had called the cops, and they took my father away. He left like a lamb. He still kept saying, 'I'm sorry.'

"They took us kids away to juvenile hall and put us in the care of a psychiatric nurse. They were all trying to be nice to us, but we didn't want to be there. Only my brother got to stay out, because he was eighteen. I'm the youngest. I was only twelve years old then.

"In a while they put all of us in different foster homes, but I kept running away. I hated the foster homes – no family, no friends, all strangers. All I wanted to do was kill my father. I didn't want to live either. I wanted to be with my beautiful mother in heaven.

"I came back to the old neighborhood and started sleeping in the park at night. I'd soak an old blanket with paint thinner and glue, put it over my head, and wrap myself in it tight. The paint thinner and the glue got me all relaxed. I could sleep and not feel that horrible pain of what happened to our family. Often the cops found me and brought me back to the foster home, but I'd just run away again."

"Where do you live now, Mousy?"

"With my brother and sister. They are adults now. They both have jobs, so we all live together. The two older ones support us younger ones. Miss, do you think that all that glue-sniffing messed up my head?"

"No, Mousy, you're doing fine. It just takes time to heal such terrible pain."

What words of comfort are there to help a child in this condition? We teachers are not taught this in our teacher training classes. What kind of teaching strategy can reach a child like Mousy?

Through my years of teaching I have met many deeply hurt students and felt totally inadequate to help them. These students have been labeled the "hard-core," the dropouts." They are the problem children who take up the teacher's and administrator's time. We warn them; we discipline then; we try to teach them about personal responsibility; we transfer them; and we expel them. Then they become a problem for the juvenile justice system and for society. If they are unlucky enough and don't meet anyone who will step in with loving and caring intervention, they will become the "stalkers," the stranglers," the "rapists," the "massacrers."

We have them all in our classrooms when they are little boys, young teenagers. They sit there and cry out for help with many irritating acts and much antisocial behavior. We send them to counselors, who get tired of dealing with them, because they are overworked.

We kick them out, because there is a limit to human patience. Let the cops deal with them. These kids don't listen anyway. They are stubborn. They need to learn the hard way. We wash our hands of them. We must pay attention to the good, deserving children in our schools. Why reward the troublemakers with our good energy?

Years later attention will be paid. People will gasp in horror at the unspeakable atrocities committed. We will buy newspapers and spend hours reading stories and watching the news. Police will spend thousands of hours apprehending them. We will spend thousands of dollars and thousands of hours in courtrooms, and then we will spend tens of thousands of dollars housing their bodies. Yes, attention will be paid one day, but only after many innocent victims have lost their lives and the human soul has sunk to another lower level of degradation.

We, the educators, have a great chance to help these children, but we need the public's support. We already pay for their transportation and for their free lunches. Now we must find a way to help the confused, abused, and troubled souls of our young people, because their numbers are growing.

At one point in his life a boy will say to himself the same thing José said to me: "Miss, I don't know whether to be a good boy or a bad boy."

There is a sensitive time, usually around fourteen, when boys make that decision consciously or, most likely, subconsciously. They need caring, aware adults around to help them make the right decisions. Then all of us will win, and the attention we give will bear wonderful fruit.

After my talk with Mousy, I realized that I was not adequately prepared to help these students with severe emotional problems. The emphasis on learning was too rational, too intellectual. Most of the students did not have problems with their intelligence; their problems were emotional. Some had been hurt to the core of the their soul. No amount of intellectual drill will produce any changes. These students need healing, caring relationships with adults, but most of us have just enough energy to deal with our own problems.

However, in one class at U.C.L.A. I did learn how to be a more effective reading teacher, so I continued with the program. One method that worked with many students was the "ORAL-AURAL METHOD". A student would dictate his story into a microphone, then I would type it and the student would read his own story.

Learning about Mousy's experience encouraged me to establish closer relationships with other students. I particularly wanted to reach Mary, La Wina. One morning the subject of astrology came up, and I asked Mary when her birthday was. She replied that it was November eighteenth.

"Really?" was my surprised reply. "That's my birthday too. Of course, a few years earlier. We have a lot in common, Mary. We're both Scorpios. Let's celebrate our birthday together. We'll have a party with cake and punch for the whole class."

All the students agreed that this was a great idea. The chance discovery of our mutual birthday opened up new avenues of communication and trust.

Mary had been in my class for two months now but had done nothing. She rejected all reading materials as either too hard, too easy, or too boring. After our conversation, however, Mary took out her folder, picked up a New Practice Reader 1, and began reading. After a few moments she came to my desk to inform me that the book was too easy for her. I handed her the next level reader, and she settled right down to work. I was completely amazed that such a chance conversation should have so positive an effect when all my other strategies had failed.

Mary read to me every day, and soon I discovered that she had problems decoding beginning and ending consonant blends. After assigning the Troubleshooter series, Mary's reading increased to the sixth-grade level from an initial second-grade level. This apparent progress encouraged her greatly.

Mary was now seventeen years old and had been out of school for four years. She told me that she had been a good student in grammar school, because she had nice teachers, but in junior high her problems began, because she was sick a lot and also her mother did not want her to go to school because of gang activities there. Her transcripts for the two years of junior high did show straight failures.

Her progress in reading skills amazed me. She decided to stay for summer school and often worked at my desk. During the summer one of Mary's close friends' sister was murdered by a rival gang. Brother Fernando knew about Mary's progress, and he asked her to read part of the funeral mass. The whole community was proud of Mary that evening.

Shortly Doctor Blake hired Mary as my teaching aide. She began holding reading circles with some of her classmates. I encouraged Mary to go on to college and become a teacher, but she said that she did not have the patience to work with all those "brats."

We had a few successes to keep us hanging in there, but most of the students had such short attention spans and seemed so full of nervous energy that they found silence in the classroom quite unbearable. Someone had to be talking or causing some kind of disturbance.

Studies have shown that anxiety interferes with the learning process. The reduction of anxiety became a major task. We tried to establish an accepting therapeutic environment in order to reduce anxiety. We thought perhaps some background music would relax them and give them enough noise so that they would not have to create their own. They had been used to constant television and stereos, so that they found silence to be most disturbing.

Unfortunately, I had not foreseen the new problems this idea would pose. When I announced to the class that we could listen to the radio if it would help them work better, they all agreed that music would help them to concentrate better. As could have been expected, not everyone liked the same music. The bolder ones would run up and change the station. That would cause others to shout in protest. When I threatened to cancel the music as a bad idea, they agreed not to fight over which station to listen to. This seemed to work for a while until a new student arrived.

Days before I got the news from Maria that "Keller" would soon be coming to our school. She said that his probation officer had decided to release him to his parents under the condition that he attend the Barrio School every day.

I asked Maria why they called him "Killer."

She said, "It's because he has an uncontrollable temper, and he goes crazy."

However, I was certain that a probation officer was wise enough not to release a dangerous person out of custody.

Sure enough, one morning soon Killer did arrive in my class. He did not look particularly ominous. He was fairly short, muscular with curly black hair, and quieter than the rest of the students. There seemed to be some brooding intensity about him. He was quite an accomplished artist and spent most of his time drawing pictures of low-ride cars and provocative chola girls. He liked listening to the radio. The music seemed to have a relaxing effect on him.

As one particular song came on, he went to the radio and turned up the volume quite loud. I just lowered it a bit. Again he turned it up, giving me a dark look full of resentment.

Brother Fernando had been observing this interaction between us. He came over and turned down the volume again.

Killer lunged at him and grabbed him by his clerical collar. "You mother fucker, just because you wear your collar backwards doesn't give you the right to push me around. You're no better than any of us. I see you flirting around with the girls at the parish. You phony!"

We all froze in silence. Brother Fernando was much taller than Killer. I was sure he could handle this.

One of the mothers came running over and touched Killer lightly on the shoulder. "Now listen, mi ijo, Brother Fernando isn't trying to hurt you. He's here to help all of you. The music was too loud for studying. We've all worked too hard to get you a school. Now don't mess it up. Apologize to the brother!"

The boy released his grip on the brother's collar and sat down.

Connie began speaking to the class. She reminded them that this school had helped all of them. It had helped to keep them out of jail. The mothers were receiving more welfare money because they were in school.

I was completely shocked by the boy's behavior. No wonder they called him "Killer." What happened to all the respect these students were supposed to have for the church?

Some member of the community considered the school a great success. Mainly it appeared that the local crime rate had dropped appreciably. The kids spend more time in a controlled environment and less time out in the streets. They had to get to bed fairly early in order to get to class on time.

Rosas, however, was becoming more and more disillusioned with the students. He was an adult schoolteacher and accustomed to highly motivated adult students. He was not used to wasting his time and energy in maintaining a semblance of discipline. Their immature and self-destructive behavior also irritated him. He decided that they were too immature to appreciate what they had, what the community so strenuously fought for. He also resented the fact that so many people dropped in anytime and claimed credit for the success of the school when we were the ones on the front lines struggling to make the school relevant to the students, to motivate them, to encourage them.

One day toward the end of the school year, Rosas told me that he was tired of working two jobs. He said that if he was going to try to save people, he was going to stop working in a "cemetery" and devote his time to working in a "hospital," where people still have a chance to live and to get well.

I found his figures of speech quite concrete and shocking. What was he implying about our students? How would the community take this? He was the teacher whom they had selected for their children.

After three months of working with them, Rosas decided that he had enough of their laziness and immaturity.

When I told Doctor Blake about Rosas' decision, his matter-of-fact reply was, "Well, what did you expect? He's used to teaching adult school. There are no discipline problems with adults. We knew he wouldn't last. Now we can put an experienced teacher in there who is used to dealing with this type of student. They won't be screaming about a <u>Chicano</u> anymore. This is not a <u>Chicano</u> problem or a black problem. This is a human problem. It's a problem of a great shift in our society. It's a problem of the industrial revolution, of families being disrupted, a rural society changed into an industrial, urban society. Our values have changed. We have too much leisure time but not the high consciousness to use it wisely. Too much leisure coupled with low consciousness has always driven people to self-destruct. Gandhi knew that."

"I agree with you, Doctor Blake, but how do we raise people's consciousness?"

"You're asking too many good questions, Elsa. Through education, of course. Don't worry. I have somebody in mind to work with you during summer school. Since we just opened in March, the board approved the money for summer school. The community is happy with their school, and we want to keep the community happy."

The parents and students were terribly disappointed when Rosas informed them that he was resigning as their teacher, but holding two jobs put a strain on his family relationships. His wife and daughters felt neglected by his devotion to two jobs. The community understood his reasons for leaving, especially when he told them that he would remain to be their counselor and friend. He especially encouraged the older students to register at the skills center to learn a valuable trade.

The students readily accepted the new teacher, Brent. He was tall, handsome, young, and single. The girls especially liked to flirt with him. The boys kept their loyalty to Rosas, but they accepted Brent, because he knew how to relate to them.

Chapter Three

WHO KILLED RONNIE?

The plight of Mousy touched me deeply. With Christmas approaching, I wanted to do something more for the students besides teaching them academic subjects.

Escrow was about to close on my house in Burbank. I decided to donate a few hundred dollars to the newly formed P.T.A. in order to help the students with school clothes. After I approached Rita and Connie with this idea, they agreed to spend the money on Christmas presents for all the students. I left it up to the mothers as to how to spend the money, since they knew each child's material situation more than I did.

After a few days Connie informed me that they had decided to order all the students black sweatshirts with the name <u>MARIPOSA</u> emblazoned on the back in white letters. This order would cost around five hundred dollars. I found this decision truly startling. It must be what the students wanted. Was the community proud of their gang name? Did it give them all an identity, or did they consider themselves merely a youth club?

This news brought to my realization that the "gang" problem was much more complex than I could comprehend. Did these kids actually have community support, or were the parents obeying the children?

I told Connie that with the money that was left over, I wanted her to buy Mousy some new school clothes. She agreed to take him and others shopping. The students were very proud of their new "club" shirts. It seemed to give them a certain dignity and pride.

In early January, on a quiet Saturday afternoon, I received a most shocking phone call from Connie's daughter Della. "Elsa, they killed Ronnie. The Rock killed Ronnie yesterday afternoon at five o'clock. He just came home from juvenile hall an hour ago. He was wearing his new sweatshirt with <u>MARIPOSA</u> written on the back. He was just walking to a neighbor's house when a car drove up, and somebody fired at him from close range. They got him between the eyes. The ambulance came and took him to the hospital, but he died a few hours later. He lost too much blood.

"Some little kids were playing outside, and they saw Ronnie fall. They saw the blood gushing from his head, his mouth and nose. You know, he was only sixteen years old. The kids saw the men in the car. They saw the one in the back seat wearing dark glasses and a headband. That's the one who fired the shot. His parents don't have any insurance, so we girls are collecting for his funeral. Could you come?"

"I'm on my way," I said.

When I arrived on Mariposa Street where Ronnie lived and died, I was met by my students who were going from house to house collecting for Ronnie's casket. Even though the people there were considered to be among the poorest in East Los Angeles, they all contributed. Grief, shock, and disbelief were registered on their young faces.

Ronnie's friends were sitting on the steps on Ronnie's house. They were not talking much, but there was a sense of solidarity, a sense of shared grief. It struck me then that friendship is about the only positive aspect in their lives. This is one area of their lives where they have experienced satisfaction and some sense of success. As their teacher at the Barrio School, I had become familiar with their chronic school failures, their conflict with the police, and their early acquaintance with jail, but friendship was a source of nurturing and positive feelings.

I was hesitant to enter Ronnie's house. What does one say to a mother who has lost her second son in three years to senseless gang murders? When I entered with a neighbor, the living room was crowded with relatives and friends. Rita, the mother, welcomed us with warm hugs.

The crying welled up again as each new person who entered expressed his sorrow. How can words express the intense grief etched on a mother's face, the eyes expressing a pain old yet new?

Ronnie's father sat in back of the room, a handsome, hard-working man. His eyes, red from crying, showed that he had not slept for a long time. He was quiet throughout the visit. What could his thoughts have been? Perhaps he was thinking of the reasons that his family came to this country. Perhaps he was thinking of the dreams he had for himself and later for his sons, both now dead through gang violence. What had happened to all these wonderful hopes and dreams for a better future in a new land? Who killed the dreams? Who killed Ronnie?

Was it the inherent evil of human nature?

Was it the frustration and failure of barrio life?

Was it the dominant society who is aware yet lets these conditions develop and grow?

I experienced a sense of guilt over Ronnie's death. What if I had not donated this money and Ronnie had not worn the shirt? Maybe he would not have been such a walking target and would still be alive – but why didn't the mothers foresee this eventuality?

After Ronnie's funeral the atmosphere in the barrio became very tense. All were set for more reprisals. The brothers at Soledad Church worked very hard to keep tempers down and to preach the lessons of brotherly love and <u>Viva La Raza</u>.

Community members felt it would be unsafe to continue with the Barrio School. The students, they insisted, were just a bunch of sitting ducks for more gang warfare. We were asked to move to another location, not so close to an elementary school.

It was decided to hold classes for them at the skills center, interspersed with the adult students. This way Rosas and I still would be their teachers as well as of the other adult students. This arrangement worked for a while, until the adults started complaining about some of the immature disruptive behavior of the high school students. Eventually only those over eighteen could remain if they were serious about their education. The rest were encouraged to go back to regular school.

So ended the experiment of a community-based school tailored to the needs of students with special problems. Was it a success? I really don't know. It all depends on whom you talk to. It was a success in the sense that we all learned lessons about ourselves, about the complexity of the problems we faced, about our inadequacy in dealing with them. In my opinion, I would evaluate the program as "too little and too late."

If we really want to help troubled youngsters, we must begin in junior high, if not sooner, but in junior high their problems become more apparent. The child is not so tied to the home. The schools and other social agencies could then step in to intensify their efforts to help the child. As their school records began coming in, it became very clear that the failure process intensified in the seventh, eight, and ninth grades. In those grades most students had failures and "unsatisfactories."

After being out of school for three or four years when their habits of failure had become entrenched, then they were given the chance at sixteen to attend continuation schools. Meanwhile, the sensitive years between thirteen and sixteen are totally wasted. We must look into the rationale as to why the law was written this way. If we had better and more specialized school and community programs, we would not have overcrowded prisons or juvenile halls. The prevention of human misery would be inestimable, not only to the juveniles but to their potential victims.

Recently the school records of the suspected "Night Stalker" have been publicized. It became apparent that his problems were clearly evident to the community at age fourteen, but we let eleven years slip by. Look at the attention the man was getting after he committed the murders.

34

Chapter Four

THE DIVERSION PROJECT

"Street people helping street people" was the idea behind the diversion project in Los Angeles. Since white middle-class Americans have demonstrated an inability to deal with the problems of black youth, it was assumed that the "blind could lead the blind."

This agency was funded by the juvenile justice system and administered through Teen Post, Inc. Three such programs were initiated based on government surveys of the three highest crime areas in Los Angeles. This was to be a consortium effort with the probation department, police, schools, and various social service agencies working together to divert young gang members from a life of crime and self-destruction to one of self-respect and productivity.

The Los Angeles Diversion Project was comprised of a director, assistant director, two senior counselors, two street workers, and an executive secretary as well as a receptionist. The director of the project – "Big Sal," as he liked to be called – was on leave for one year from the probation department. Doctor Blake, the administrator of the Los Angeles Continuation Education Schools, was approached by the director to open a branch of this school. The project would supply the "dropouts" if Doctor Blake could supply a strong black male teacher to teach the "hard-core" gang members, someone who could relate to these students.

"Unfortunately," Doctor Blake replied, "I don't have a strong black male teacher available right now, and even if I knew of one, I doubt that he would want to teach in a small storefront school, but I have a qualified small white female teacher whom I can give you. She is experienced with working in continuation schools and especially with gang-oriented youth."

"No way will I be responsible for a white female teacher with our hard-core clients," Big Sal insisted. "With the type of students we have, she won't last a day."

Doctor Blake, however, reiterated that he knew his teachers and what they were capable of doing. If Sal did not want this particular teacher who was available, then unfortunately he had no one else at the moment. Later Doctor Blake informed me that Big Sal threatened to resign the directorship unless he were given the proper staff.

High-level meetings were held, and it was decided by the Teen Post administration that I would be hired on a trial basis. Doctor Blake offered me the job and explained the situation. He told me that he had confidence in me to do a good job.

This offer sounded like a great opportunity for growth to me. I looked forward to working with so many agencies. What lessons and what insight I might gain from this experience! Naively I assumed that all these people would be "experts" in the field of diverting young people from lives of crime to those of productive citizenship.

The diversion project had officially already been in operation for several months, yet no other agency had joined the consortium. It was high time to get the classroom started.

When the time came for me to meet with the director and his staff, I was quite apprehensive knowing his frame of mind. I knew, however, that I should not take this personally. Mister Thomas, the director, no doubt had his philosophical reasons for his opinion. Eventually I hope to be able to persuade Mister Thomas that I could handle the job, that sex and color were not as important as attitude and conviction. My motto at the time was, "It's personality, not nationality, that counts."

The building was located in South Central Los Angeles, a clean business and commercial area. Once the building had been a beauty outlet as well as a beauty parlor. Now the inside had been divided into small, newly painted offices. I felt impressed by the clean middle-class neighborhood with tree-lined streets and prosperous shopping centers. It was not at all what I expected a "ghetto" to look like.

My heart pounded nervously as I approached the new work assignment. How would the people react to me? Would they be unfriendly or even hostile? Did they hate "Whitey?"

As I entered, an attractive young receptionist greeted me with the usual, "May I help you?"

"I'm Elsa Cummins, your new teacher sent by the board of education. I have an appointment with Mister Sal Thomas."

She checked her calendar. "That's right, Miss Cummins. Just have a seat. I'll call Mister Thomas. My name is Peggy. I'm the receptionist here."

"Pleased to meet you, Peggy. Just call me Elsa. This certainly is a nice building, all cool and freshly painted."

"Yes, it's pretty nice, but it's been very quiet around here. We've been waiting for a teacher before we started calling in our clients."

"Well, here I am, your new teacher."

Presently Mister Thomas appeared.

No wonder they call him "Big Sal", I thought.

He approached me, all smiling and fatherly. "So you're the little lady Doctor Blake sent. He recommended you highly for this job. You sure don't look tough or threatening to me, Miss Cummins."

"I hope not, Mister Thomas. Teachers who look tough and threatening don't last very long with the type of student we'll be dealing with, because then they have to prove they are tougher and meaner than the teacher. Students aren't threatened by me at all. I act respectfully toward them, and most of them treat me with respect."

This seemed an appropriate time to interject my philosophy of teaching and also good human relations in general.

"We'll get along just fine, Miss Cummins. Step into my office. I'd like you to meet my secretary, Jane."

After the introductions, Sal smiled and asked, "Are you ready to go to lunch, ladies? Where do you wish to go?"

"How about your favorite place, Sal?" Jane asked.

"Great!" was Sal's enthusiastic reply.

"We'll show Elsa some real soul food."

"You ever had soul food?" Sal asked mischievously.

"No," I said, "but I'm willing to experience some new food."

We had a friendly, amicable lunch. The food was delicious. I had oxtails, yams, greens, and cornbread. They laughed at my great appetite and my enjoyment of the flavorful yams. I felt comfortable with Jane and Sal. It appeared that they liked me too. If there was any undercurrent of disapproval or rejection of me, I certainly did not feel it.

When we returned to the office, Sal asked me when I could begin work. I told him that tomorrow would be fine with me, because it would take me all afternoon to collect books and ma-

terials from the board of education. We would need books for
all subjects – English, reading, math, American history, etc. We
needed reading materials for many levels. From my experience
we would have students with a wide range of skills, anywhere
from fifth- to twelfth-grade reading levels. Most of them would
probably fall in the fourth- to sixth-grade range.

"Good. We'll see you tomorrow sometime," Sal said. "By
the way, do you need someone to help you clean up the classroom?"

"Sure, that would be appreciated. Can you get me someone?" I asked.

"Of course. I'll have two of my street workers help you. You
all might as well get acquainted. You'll be working closely with
them. They're just a couple of street kids I'm helping to rehabilitate. They're a couple of years older than the kids you'll be
working with. I believe the way to rehabilitate young punks is
to give them some responsibility for other people. Hal and Leo,
the two street workers, will be responsible for those students of
yours. They'll see to it that they show up on time. They'll call
the parents if they're truant or you have any discipline problems.
Let us handle all of that. You just teach.

"Those kids will have to mind, or else they'll have to deal
with me. They know they can't bullshit me. They can't con a
con. I'm wise to all that. Hell, I've been one of them at their
age. Why, at the age of fourteen I had to leave home for being
accused of killing a white man. Now nobody knows who did it,
but in those days just to be accused made you guilty, so I had to
be on the run at fourteen and learn about survival on the streets.

"I've have to fend for myself ever since that age, but all
along I've had women helping me. At fifteen I had me a woman
who was forty-five. She made sure I went to school. She cooked

for me, and I made sure she was always satisfied. These kids know I'm not jivin'."

Big Sal pulled up his shirt and showed me a large old scar in his massive stomach. "I've been shot and wounded and survived. I know the life of these young hoods. You can't be soft with them. So, maybe the two of us will work out just fine. You can give them the mother image, and I'll give them the strong father image that most of them don't have. You know, most of our kids are on welfare, and most of them don't have fathers. They have welfare mothers who have so many problems of their own, they can't deal with their children's too. These kids get away with anything, because no adult has bothered to give them much guidance. Maybe they got a few slaps or even beatings, but not much help. They need a firm hand, and I'm the one who's gonna give it to them"

That afternoon I went to see Doctor Blake to thank him for selecting me for this assignment. Then I stopped at the book room and stocked up on books, reading kits, and various supplies. I also brought some posters to decorate the classroom walls.

The next morning I eagerly arrived with the new books and supplies. The two street workers, Leo and Hal, helped me carry in everything and clean up the shelves. They seemed like a couple of high-school students, and I had no problem relating to them.

Mrs. Green and Mister Loos, the two head counselors, came in to admire the classroom. It was beginning to shape up, especially after the posters were on the walls.

Mrs. Green was an attractive mother of three teenaged children, all attending school there. She was a welfare mother and a long-time friend of Mister Thomas. He wanted her on his staff, because he felt that she knew about the problems of our students as well as their parents. Therefore she would be in an excellent position to help them. I liked Mrs. Green right away and felt that we would become friends.

Mister Loos acted a bit too friendly and flirtatious. He was a balding middle-age man with a roving eye for anything in a skirt. He cornered me when I was alone in the classroom and asked me to go out with him that evening. When I refused, he gave me the old "You don't want to go out with me because I'm black" routine.

"What makes you think I'm prejudiced?" I asked. "For all you know, I might have a black husband or boyfriend already."

"One isn't enough, baby. You can always add me to your list. I'll make it good to you. You'll see. I'm a man of great experience."

"I'm sure you are, Mister Loos, but if I went out with every man who asked me, I'd be in a different profession. As you can see, I'm teaching instead."

"You wait and see," was his sly reply. "I'm gonna get you yet."

"I'm sure that'll never happen, Loos," I flipped back.

A few days after this conversation, Loos asked me whether I had ever seen the movie "Shampoo" with Warren Beatty. I told him that I had seen it.

"Well, that hairdresser played by Warren reminded me of myself. Before Sal gave me this job, I was a hairdresser, and baby, I'd do their hair during the day and do them at night. I drove myself ragged, so many ladies requested my services. I couldn't turn them down. I did so many women that I ended up having a nervous breakdown. A lot of husbands were after me with guns. My wife finally left, and I fell apart for a while. Now I have my own place. I don't have to worry about getting shot by a jealous husband. The women come knocking on my door if they want me to do them."

"Loos," I asked, surprised, "how did you ever get to be a counselor? Do you have a degree?"

"Degree? Degree in what? I have a degree in human nature. I'm an expert in ghetto life. Those superior fools with degrees are laughable. Big Sal knows what I can do. We have been friends since college days. Sal is no fool. He knows this is a white man's world, and he knows you have to play the white man's game to get over. He got himself an education. He believes in that. He played football in college. Because he was so good, he was signed up with a professional team. Sal's made a lot of money. When he got this program, he wanted me along because he don't forget his friends. Sal knows I'm nobody's fool either. I know these street punks. They can't run their games on me like they do on them fools with their fancy degrees. They know I'll knock their heads in if they don't behave."

Loos really tried to impress me with his superior insight into the ghetto psychology. Mercifully Mister Thomas entered my classroom to announce that a close friend of his from college days, a Doctor Perry, had arrived from Texas for a short visit.

Doctor Perry had seen my classroom the previous night and was impressed by the environment, because he could not tell whether the teacher was black or white. Doctor Perry was a consultant for several federal programs as well as various school districts. Through many years of evaluating programs and schools, he was able to tell the race and general attitude of the person inhabiting the environment. Apparently he helped Sal put his mind at ease about me. He had liked what he saw so far and wanted to meet me.

The secretary phoned the classroom to let us know that Doctor Perry was here to take us all out to lunch. After meeting all the streetwise staff, I was highly impressed by Doctor Perry. He was a man of great intelligence, education, and insight, perhaps on the level of Doctor Martin Luther King.

He convinced Mister Thomas that I would do all right with the students. The two of us working together might strike the needed balance. Sal could provide the much-needed discipline, while I would provide empathy and understanding. Our unique talents pooled together would make this program work. I was delighted by Doctor Perry's evaluation of me. His confidence gave me much-needed moral support, especially after meeting some of the other staff.

Chapter Five

INSTRUCTION BEGINS

The agency registered about twenty students to attend classes in the newly set-up classroom. Instruction was totally individualized. It was more like tutoring. Each student was given an oral reading test as well as a math test. After his reading level was determined, the student was given four contracts, one in English or reading improvement, one in math, American history, and social studies.

On the first day about ten students arrived. After the usual introduction and explanation of the program, I asked students to write a page telling me something about their previous education and family life. I tried to avoid my previous mistake of asking for an "autobiography." While the other students were busily writing, I called individual students for their oral reading tests.

The school day was divided into two two-hour periods with a twenty-minute break between classes. Students could work on any subject they wanted and for as long as they wanted. As soon as the work of the contract was completed, they received their grades and their credits. This system motivated many students to put forth some effort. They were made to feel that they were not competing with anyone for grades. They were just growing at their own speed.

Some students worked hard for a "completion slip." At the end of each semester they were issued regular report cards. Many students had such poor study habits and such poor self-images that they wasted a lot of time. Here the counselors and street workers were supposed to apply added pressure. They often reminded them that their welfare checks to their families would be cut off if they did not achieve in school.

Classes were to begin at nine o'clock, because this was the time when the Diversion Project was to open, but usually no one arrived until nine-ten or nine-fifteen, forcing me and many students to wait outside. I brought this up at one of our many staff meetings, reminding them that we are supposed to set an example to our students about the importance of punctuality.

This made Big Sal laugh. "I see you never heard of C.P. time."

"C.P. time. What's that?" I asked, surprised.

They all looked at me and laughed.

"You see," Big Sal said, "there is white people's time, and there is colored people's time – and we're on colored people's time."

They all roared with laughter about this inside joke. I had to admit I never heard of C.P time, but since I was on board-of-education time, I had better begin on their time, or else we might get no more time. I did not think the board had much of a sense of humor. They were concerned about public relations and a good image in the community.

Big Sal definitely understood white people's time and decided to give me a key, so we would not have to stand around in the morning and get unfavorable public attention. Many times I had to open the office and even answer the phone.

The first commandment in continuation education is to build self-esteem, confidence, and constantly foster a positive self-image. Never ridicule or belittle a student, but always encourage and praise any effort expended toward achievement. Most students thrive on individual attention. This can be done in a classroom of twenty or less with a teacher who is flexible and compassionate as well as trained in the subject matter to be taught.

Some students wanted to be left alone and work on their own, while others constantly asked for help. I remember two students in particular who were intelligent but for some reason did not learn to read in elementary or in junior high school.

Often breakthroughs happen under the most unusual and spontaneous circumstances. Joe, a tall, husky young man, hoped to play football in senior high school but was not accepted on the team, because he could not read. He was one of the most hyperactive and energetic youngsters who really tried my patience every day.

One day he announced, "Monday is my birthday. What will you give me?"

"What do you want, Joe?" I asked.

Often I brought in birthday cake for students who announced their birthdays in advance.

"I'd like a pot of chili, miss. Man, do I like chili."

"Really? That's great. Chili is one of my specialties. I hope you like the way I make it."

Next Monday morning when I brought the chili, Joe was genuinely surprised and elated. After that time he accepted me as a real teacher. He felt comfortable enough to settle down and concentrate on learning to read. They never taught us at university about the "chili method" of teaching reading. There must be a right key to open any child's mind.

I was as amazed as Joe when he learned to read, and fast too. When the other students were busy with their work, Joe would sit next to me on a Naugahide couch and read to me. We began with primary readers. I corrected him when he misread a word, explaining the rules of phonics as he went along. Sometimes I would read a few paragraphs to him when he became tired. We both felt comfortable doing this. . It reminded me of the times when my children were small and I read to them.

Joe advanced so fast, he was convinced he would be accepted by the football coach and be able to go back to his regular high school. When the day came for him to leave, we were very proud of him. He often came to visit us and to thank me for teaching him to read. I pointed out to him that he learned to read because he really wanted to. He had a goal that was important to him.

Another student, Derek, who wanted to learn to read in order to pass his driver's test, was on the "ten most wanted" list for gang activity. One day he stayed after school and wrote me the following letter:

Dear Miss Cummins,

You are one of the best teachers I could ever have. In a way I think you should have been my teacher in the first grade. I believe if you would have been my teacher in the first grade, I might be on my way on being president or any other dream like a lawyer, doctor, or dentist, or any other kind of career that I want. This is one of the best years of my life at school. Because down the line in school I haven't learned anything. Since the day I stepped into your class on 2/9/75, I began to learn. Now it is 6/9/75, and I can read the newspapers, comic books, and Jet magazine. So these were the things I couldn't read.

By Derek Baille
Age 17

This was written after Derek passed his written examination for a driver's license. His joy and enthusiasm touched me deeply. It made all the effort, all the battles with the staff over "philosophy" worthwhile.

Derek was very proud of himself. He told my shyly, "Miss, the only thing I could read before was 'Fuck You' written all over the walls in our neighborhood. Now I could read and understand the test."

Often a student would touch my hair and hands, asking, "What color are you anyway?"

"What do you mean?" I would ask in amazement, and hold my hand next to his. "What color do I look like? It's white or beige."

"No, you're not white."

They were so sure of that, I began to wonder what really was behind the question.

"How many white people do you know?" I asked.

"Well, the police and the probation officers. They're white."

"Maybe you're talking more about attitude than color," I replied. "There are all kinds of white people, just like there are all kinds of black people. Certain professions have certain attitudes because of their experiences. As I told you before, personality is much more important than nationality."

Apparently I did not fit into their stereotype of "Whitey"; therefore, I could not be white. I took it as a compliment and a sign of their acceptance.

Often I would say, "You're right. I'm a mixture of white, Chinese, and some black."

They were satisfied with that answer. I realized how limited their experience of life had been to their own ghetto.

We saw the need to expand that experience. The agency, with the approval of the school, planned various field trips for the students. We took them to the beach, the county Museum of Science and Industry, and hiking in Griffith Park. We also planned a trip to Universal Studios. The students all looked forward to this trip with great excitement.

On the day of departure we all sat around anxiously waiting for the bus to arrive to take us on our long-awaited trip. At first I thought perhaps the bus was operating on C.P. time. Finally one of the counselors called the bus company and informed us about the "misunderstanding" of the date of the trip, which they thought was to be next week.

This was the final straw that broke the camel's back. I lost my charm and professional manner when confronted with another blunder.

"What this program needs around here is leadership," I blurted out, looking at the assistant director. "Too many of you are just standing around joking, laughing, and plain doing nothing. This program is a real joke. If it weren't for the school, there really would be nothing here. Even the students are talking about it. Let's pool our own cars and take them ourselves. There aren't that many here."

"No, we can't do that. We have to answer the phone. We can't close the place down. Somebody from the main office might call."

"Appearances, appearances, that's all any of you think about. The secretary could handle the phone by herself."

They were unanimously against the idea. Big Sal was out of town. I wondered how he would have handled this.

"If you can't take them," I said, "then I'll take all who will fit in my car."

"It'll all be your responsibility if you do that," the assistant director informed me.

I asked the students how many wanted to go with me to the studio. About six raised their hands. I informed them that unfortunately there was room for only four in my car. They argued among themselves who was to go. As it turned out, the four who considered themselves leaders came along.

We piled into the car in great spirits. After a lengthy discussion as to who would ride "shotgun," Lenny ended up sitting in the front seat. As we drove off, he lightly placed his hand on my knee. I moved my knee away.

From the back seat Willy shouted, "Cut it out, Lenny! She's nice enough to take us in her own car, burning her own gas. Can't you see she's a real lady?"

"Thank you, Willy. Let's just all have a good time and stay together when we get there. Don't smoke any weed or do anything to get noticed or get yourselves arrested like the trouble we had at the job fair. We'll get enough looks already – one white woman with four black men – so just be real gentlemen."

We all enjoyed Universal Studios tremendously. We toured the wardrobe and props departments. Willy especially enjoyed the performance by several stunt men. The audience even got a chance to perform in a skit. Willy and Michael volunteered. They really made the audience laugh with their acting. It ended up being a truly happy day for all of us. On the way back we turned on the radio, and we all sang along.

When we got back to the black neighborhood, a white policeman was following us.

Willy noticed him. "I bet he's gonna stop us."

"Why?" I asked.

"Because he sees a white woman with four black men. I bet he thinks we're kidnapping you and making you drive us somewhere."

"You're kidding," I said in surprise.

Sure enough, the policeman flashed his lights. I pulled over.

He cautiously approached the car. "May I see your driver's license?"

I pulled out my license.

"Is everything all right, lady?" he asked.

"Yes, sir," I replied.

"Your rear right tire is pretty bald. Better have it replaced before you have a blowout."

"That's right, Officer. I'm planning to do that soon. Thank you."

"Have a good day, ma'am."

"See what I told you?" Willy said after the officer had gone.

"You sure know a lot about cops, Willy."

"Yeah, I'm considered a juvenile delinquent. They know me around here. They're always messing with me."

When I got back, the assistant director was still at the office. He seemed relieved that all had gone well and that we came back in high spirits.

I had been told that these young people were the "gang-bangers" who assaulted teachers and had no respect for authority. They did not respect adults or any authority figures. They could not be controlled by their parents or teachers. All they understood was force. I really did not know exactly what to expect from these students, but I did know that all human beings respond favorably to warmth, friendship, and praise.

When a student turned in a good paper, I would write a big red <u>A</u> on the top. At first I was totally amazed to see these so-called tough guys with their black leather jackets beaming with pride, showing their papers to fellow classmate. They were thoroughly pleased with themselves when their received good grades. Somehow I believed that they would be totally indifferent and uninterested about achievement in school.

Many students sat next to me and read orally to show me how they had improved. Often I actually felt like a mother with all those children in my care. When one spends four hours a day for many moths with a small group, one tends to become more involved and closer on a human level. The roles become overlapped. I was not only their teacher but also their counselor, mother, friend, and sometimes chauffeur.

The girls would show me pictures of their babies and sometimes bring them to class to show them off. This is when I became aware of the skin-shade hierarchy among blacks. When a girl had a light-skinned baby, they all made comments about the pretty light skin the baby had. A young woman with light skin was considered a beauty and sought after for dates. I overheard some girls talk about a new boy who had just arrived. Their comment was that he was too black and ugly. This constant reference to skin tone was news to me.

I brought along a reading kit dealing with black history and another one about famous black people, believing these kits would be very popular. They were, but only with some students.

Others rejected them, saying, "I don't want to read nothing about those niggers. I already know about them."

It appeared to me that students with a more positive self-image enjoyed reading the biographies of black people, but those with deeper emotional problems seemed to reject them.

It seemed to me that a great deal of self-hatred was involved in these rejections. Even though this self-rejection comes from living in a discriminating white culture, not all students suffered from this poison. This destructive force in their lives must ultimately spill over into society. I began to understand the "Black is Beautiful" movement.

This new discovery would not leave my thoughts. I had to discuss this with someone, not just from an intellectual standpoint but from real experience if possible. The next time Doctor Perry and I had lunch. I brought up the problem even though I was afraid to offend him or to sound racist. Nevertheless, I wanted his opinion. He would either confirm or deny my "discovery." I did not know exactly how to approach the subject.

Finally, after a pause in our conversation, I said, "Please don't be offended by what I have to say. Tell me whether I made a wrong observation. I've discovered that many of our students suffer from self-rejection, that they actually dislike their blackness."

Then I related several incidents that brought me to this conclusion.

Doctor Perry looked at me intently for a long time before he replied, "I remember when I was a little boy, my mother made me go to sleep with a clothespin pinching my nostrils together. She said they were too wide and that sleeping with a clothespin would give me a more attractive, narrow nose. I remember it hurt a lot physically, but the emotional pain was much more severe. I had to breathe through my mouth and couldn't fall asleep. I resented my mother for rejecting my nose. After all I inherited it from her."

His painful revelation touched me deeply. Tears welled up, and I could not swallow my food.

He continued, "I have a light-skinned brother, and our mother was always fussing over him. He was decidedly her favorite son, but I'm the one with the motivation and the education. Now she's really proud of me. I'm the one who 'got over.' My fair-skinned brother didn't even finish high school. Now he works as a clerk in a post office. You really can't blame the parents though. They only want the best for their children, and they know that their lighter-complected children have more of a chance to make it in a white society. They're less visible.

"I know a lot a black people who broke through the color line. If they have light skin, they can get a nose job, or a lip-reduction operation. Some just have their hair straightened, and presto! They can pass as Italian, Greek, or Turkish.

"It's true – dark-complected children do feel more rejected by their parents and by society. We ourselves are perpetuating a terrible evil. Once a person feels that no one cares for him, that he is inferior, that he can't achieve anything on his own, he begins to feel that he has nothing to lose. They go out and take from the people who do have something. Eventually, when they begin to hate their own life, they go out and take someone else's life.

"That's the ultimate robbery, when you rob someone of his life. I've visited prisons and observed that it's really full of very dark men. Why do you think we've started the black awareness movement? We know about the cancer that is spreading in our society. We want our young people to know that black is beautiful. We are trying to build their self-respect and a feeling of worthiness as a human being."

When we parted, I had a much deeper understanding of the feelings that many of the students struggled with. We both agreed that this destructive trend could be reversed if white society realized what pain they perpetuated through prejudice and segregation. Pain knows no boundaries. It spills at random on anyone, just like a germ or a virus. Doctor Perry encouraged me to continue with my work and not become discouraged over philosophical disagreements with the staff.

Apparently a staff meeting had been held after the students and I returned from our trip to Universal Studios to discuss my rebelliousness and unprofessional conduct. The next day I was asked to attend their staff meeting after school. These meetings were lengthy emotional debates wherein we always clashed about our basic philosophies on how to rehabilitate the "hard-core."

I walked into Sal's spacious office, where the whole staff had already assembled.

"Sit down, Elsa." Sal motioned gravely, indicating a chair reserved for me. We want to talk to you about your unprofessional conduct of yesterday. You abandoned your classroom to take a few students on a field trip. Don't you know that those four are the worst of the bunch? On their records are rapes, robberies, and even murders. I know, because I was their probation officer. Never do that again. If I had been there, I wouldn't have let you go, so part of it is also my fault.

"Actually, you're a very lucky lady to have come out of this unharmed. I could picture you as another statistic of an assaulted teacher. My program don't need this kind of publicity. We're already in trouble about being refunded, because no other agency wants to join us, and this is supposed to be a consortium – but we didn't come here to talk about that. We're here to discuss your teaching methods.

"It's clear to us that you're trying to buy their love by bringing them birthday cakes and food. Don't you know the hard-core don't know nothin' about love? They'd sell their own grandmothers just to get another fix. I know these guys. Remember, I lived on the streets. Don't you know that niggers take kindness for weakness? They take advantage of you, and you're naive enough to let them. They try to play the staff against each other. You don't even see that. You've got to be tough with them, because that's all they respect. You can see they respect me, because I'm big, black, and ugly – and I carry a gun. Another thing, you're sitting much too close to those guys."

"Too close to them?" I asked in disbelief. "I'm just helping them to read."

"You don't know about niggers," Big Sal said confidentially. "They get hot much faster than them white folks. You think you're teaching them to read, but that don't count. It's what they think that matters. Those guys will have you spread-eagled on the table, and all of them will rape you, or the ones really full of hate will also end up choking you. Believe me, I know what I'm talking about. I've been their probation officer for a long time."

I was shaking with anger and total disbelief. "Mister Thomas, you talk worse than any white racist."

He laughed out loud. "That's right, Miz Anne, because I knows niggers. Now there are black people, and there are niggers. The clients we have are niggers. What do you know about them? You go home every afternoon to your all-white neighborhood. I live with them. I see how they operate and how they think."

I looked around at the rest of the staff. Some looked serious, but some were smiling at me.

"I don't care what you think you know about these kids. You're just telling me this to scare me, because you want me to quit and run scared, but you're wrong. I'm not afraid of those boys. Nobody wants to rape me or hurt me in any way. They know I'm not their enemy. They have more sense than you or I might give them credit for."

"No, Elsa, we don't want you to quit. It's our job to warn you, because we like you. Besides, we don't want any bad publicity about this program. We've got enough problems already. Believe me, Elsa, we knows niggers," Mister Thomas said in his most sincere voice.

"Mister Thomas, I know my students too, and you're totally wrong. I'll prove it to you. They don't take kindness for weakness. They know they're physically stronger than I am. They also know that I'm here to help them. Just last week 'John Wayne' came in when I was in the back storeroom all by myself. He asked, 'Aren't you afraid to be here by yourself?' "No, John, not me. Why? Are you planning to do me something? ''No, miss." 'Well, John, that's why I'm not afraid.' We smiled at each other, and he took a carton of milk and walked back to the eating area."

I went home deeply discouraged, because Big Sal believed what he had told me. He had been a probation officer for many years, and he believed himself to be an expert on human nature, at least human nature the way it is expressed in the ghetto. He saw me merely as an idealistic outsider, a "Miz Anne," a "Mighty Whitey," as I had often been called by Mister Loos when he was angry.

I felt, however, that Big Sal's assumptions about the total evilness of our students was totally unrealistic, that he was just projecting his own experience of life. If he believed so strongly in the dark side of human nature, should he be in a position of rehabilitating these students? It was as if he had given up long ago and was just going through the motions, playing the white man's game of "getting over."

I came there to teach some academic subjects, but I learned that the "hard-core" were not so different from any of us. They wanted happiness, love, success, and appreciation just like any other human being. They were not some distorted monsters. They were still young, and a few positive experiences could still bring out their total humanity, but what would happen to them in a few years if their basic need to grow in a positive direction were not nourished and encouraged? Would they "sour, fester and explode?"

It appeared to me that Big Sal was subconsciously proud of his tough guys. They certainly were not "Uncle Toms." They gave Whitey plenty of trouble. I began to believe that he secretly admired their defiance and their fearlessness. It seemed to me that he equated it with manliness. The reception area was decorated with such old headlines as "Gang Member Stabs Bus Driver" or "Gang Members Rob and Stab Welfare Mother."

I spent a fretful night trying to understand what Big Sal had told me. How should I react to the students the next morning? Was I really naive as they said, just a bleeding heart? Was I only kidding myself and trying to play God?

The next morning I arrived before nine o'clock, and as usual, nobody was there yet. I opened up and sat down on the long, green padded bench, still wondering what I would say or do. The students started to arrive, and also as usual, they sat next to me on the long bench. Most of the students had already arrived, but so far none of the staff members were in sight.

I was unusually quiet that morning, my heart pounding nervously. Impulsively I jumped up, facing the students who had been sitting next to me.

With a shaking voice I yelled, "I've been told not to let you sit next to me, because you're planning to rape me. Is that right? And if you're not going to rape me, then you're planning to choke me. Is that right?"

They all stared at me.

"Who told you that?" John Wayne asked disgustedly. "It must be those fools who work here. Now don't you listen to them. They're no better off than we are, and they think they're gonna help us. Who do they think they are, telling us what to do?"

He and several other students spontaneously proceeded to rip those old headlines off the walls. Some walked into the classroom, took out their <u>A</u> papers, and started pinning them on the walls.

They continued taking down all the negative headlines and statistics, shouting, "This ain't us! This stuff only makes people scared of us."

Then they covered the walls with their <u>A</u> papers, yelling, "Now, <u>this is us</u>!"

I began to cry and tremble with their proclamation of their true identity. This was the validation that I had been looking for and needed to continue with my efforts. I ran to the ladies' room to control my crying.

Some girls followed me and assured me that nobody wanted to hurt me. "You don't believe them fools, do you?"

"No, I don't believe them, and I'm deeply touched to know that you don't believe those headlines about yourselves either. You know who you are and what you want to become."

When Mister Thomas arrived, he wanted to know why I allowed them to tear up the place. I told him emotionally that they were not tearing up the place. They were just tired of seeing those old headlines about them that totally misrepresented them. They wanted the community to see who they really were, and the way to show them was to bring their good grades out into the open.

Now I had my answer. Their action came spontaneously, from a deep well, reinforcing my belief that all human beings want and need positive recognition and acceptance. They were not proud to be labeled "hard-core criminals." this was not the identity that they wanted they much rather wanted the identity of achieving students.

After this dramatic display the staff and I never argued about "philosophy." We held to our own individual beliefs. Even though Big Sal looked and often acted tough, I knew he had a good heart and meant well. We just had different experiences in life.

After the students demonstrated to me in concrete terms their hopes and goal, showing me, "This is us," I wanted to world to know about it. I wanted the other agencies to come in and help these young people to become positive, constructive citizens. I began by writing a letter to Mayor Tom Bradley:

Dear Mayor Bradley:

I know how deeply you are interested in the youth of our city, especially minority youth living in the barrios and ghettos. Recently you have shown deep concern for the destruction taking place in our communities and our schools.

I am a teacher at a Diversion Project in South Central Los Angeles. My task is to provide alternative education for those who have been expelled or pushed out from the comprehensive high schools in the area. These students are considered to be the hard-core youth. I had been informed that the student body consists mainly of murderers, rapists, and robbers.

The walls of our establishment were lined with such headlines as "Gang Member Kills Bus Driver" or "Welfare Mother Raped by Gang." Today when the students arrived, several of them began to tear off these old headlines exclaiming, "This isn't us. This will only make our parents and the community afraid of us. We're sick of looking at this shit." Then they proceeded to pin their math, English, and history papers on the walls, showing off their good grades. "Now this is us," they proclaimed.

I'll never forget this emotion-charged experience as long as I live. My faith in the inherent goodness of every individual has been reaffirmed. These students are tired of identifying with crime, with defeat. With this one grand gesture they have symbolically turned away from crime and second-class citizenship; they have affirmed that they want to be first-class, that they want to be achievers and not failures and destroyers.

Their main concern is with jobs. "We want jobs" is their daily plea. After experiencing much failure and rejection in the schools, they are coming here almost every day, because they have experienced some acceptance, some success in their studies. Right now they need a helping hand from the community.

I would very much appreciate it if someone from the mayor's office came to talk with these young people, to give them a hand, to support their upward struggle, to offer them some N.Y.C. jobs if only for four hours per day.

If there is a committee on youth action, I would very much like to join it. I know that young people are sick of hostility, sick of failure, sick of rejection. They are so sick of it that they are throwing it up all over our institutions. I am closing this letter with the words of Emmet Fox:

There is no difficulty that enough love will not conquer. It makes no difference how deeply seated may be the trouble; how hopeless the outlook; how muddled the tangle; how great the mistake. A sufficient realization of love will dissolve it all. If only you could love enough, you would be the happiest, the most powerful person in the world.

Unfortunately, no reply ever came, neither in writing nor by telephone. The letter was probably scrapped, like so many other endless pleas for help. Even though I had some small successes and saw the potential for much larger ones if all segments of society pulled together, I became increasingly discouraged as the months went by with routine sameness.

No other agencies joined us. Many reasons were given for refusal to cooperate with us, but it seemed to boil down to a power struggle. Some agencies refused to work with Mister Thomas. Others had no confidence in the idea of a diversion program. Most did not want to give up their autonomy and be under the directorship of some untried agency. Eventually Mister Thomas resigned, accepting a position with the housing authority.

Mister Thomas's protege was installed as the new director. We muddled through from day to day. Nothing much was going on except the school. Mrs. Green, the girls' counselor, organized a bowling league and a fashion show, but after classes were dismissed at one p.m., the students went home. There was no professional family counseling program or job placement ever developed.

Most of the staff congregated up front by the receptionist's desk. We heard their laughter and joking around in the classroom. Sometimes there were vulgar shouting and screaming matches among the staff members.

The students often commented, "Listen to them fools up front. Here we're working, and they're getting paid."

When a staff member came up with a constructive idea, the others would not support it. There was much rivalry going on among the staff. Nobody wanted the others to look too good in front of the director.

All kinds of sexual intrigue came to the surface. Mister Loos resumed chasing me after Mister Thomas had gone. One morning he followed me upstairs, grabbed me in the hall, and kissed me. I felt like a little junior high school kid. I threatened to report his behavior to the new director.

I had a good relationship with Mrs. Green, and I confided in her about Loos's advances. Unfortunately, I did not know that the two counselors were having an intimate relationship. I realized this one morning when they both arrived at work together in Mrs. Green's car. When they came in and Loos saw me standing alone, he came right over and tried to hug and kiss me in front of Mrs. Green. Right there his destructive exploitation of women dawned on me.

I let him have it in front of all the staff. "Look, Loos, I know the kind of sick game you're playing here. You know Mrs. Green and I are friends. You just want to make her jealous of me and destroy our friendship. You want her to dislike and distrust me. You're playing a dirty game, and I'm wise to it."

His eyes bulging with rage, he snapped, "Fuck you in the ass, you white bitch. You don't know what you're talking about. You think you're Mighty Whitey around here. You don't know shit."

"Well, Loos, I knew one day your true self would really come out, and especially the way you feel about women."

I just walked away from him as the staff watched in silence.

From then on Loos stopped chasing me. We were not on speaking terms either. His prediction of, "One day I'll get you," did not come true.

Since nothing else was happening for the students, Doctor Blake decided to hire an arts and crafts teacher to come in twice a week to work with the students. We left the usual classroom and went upstairs where we had more tables to spread out.

On one of these occasions when the art teacher was there, I noticed one of the young, pretty girls was missing from the group. When I inquired where Lena was, one of the girls replied that she stayed behind in the classroom. I walked back downstairs to the classroom and found out what was keeping her. To my great shock, there sat Lena in her usual seat, with Mister Loos kneeling in front of her. Lena's blouse was unbuttoned, while Loos was intently fondling her breasts.

Loos turned around as I entered the room. Lena jumped up and ran out of the room.

I stared at Loos in utter contempt, yelling, "What are you, a child molester too? Here you are, forty-five years old, molesting a little student of fourteen! You're getting paid by the government to rehabilitate these kids, not to turn them into sexual delinquents. This is supposed to be a diversion project, and just what are you diverting this girl to?"

"Shut your mouth," he snapped in a vicious tone of voice. "You don't know what you're talking about. You call them 'young ladies' or 'my students.' That's a laugh. Them's a bunch of whores who've been walking up and down Hollywood Boulevard every night. So what if they're only fifteen? They've been fucking since they was ten years old. You don't know nothing about the ghetto, Miss High and Mighty. If you were from the ghetto, you'd know them girls are nothin' but a bunch of whores."

"But that's why you're here, to show them a better way of life, to show them respect," I said. "You're not here to exploit their innocence and their weaknesses."

"Don't you talk to me about exploitation. The white people are experts at that."

He was trying to shift his guilt onto me!

"Don't try to make yourself feel superior," I replied. "I didn't exploit any black people. I'm a peasant from Poland. We didn't own any slaves. Besides, you're confusing the issue. Since black people were exploited by whites, that doesn't make it moral that now you should exploit your own people. Suppose I call her mother?"

Loos really laughed then. "Go ahead and call her mother. Her mother will laugh in your face. She expects Lena to bring home a certain amount of money every day. She doesn't care how Lena gets it. That's one of the advantages of having a beautiful daughter. She can make money the easy way. See, you don't know nothin'. Don't come on with your puritan white values, not with me. Besides, you saw nothing. Nothing! I'll make you look like a real fool if you mention anything to anybody. Got the picture, Miz Anne?"

"Yes, Loos, I get the picture, and it's an ugly one."

When I reported this incident to one of the school administrators, his reply really amazed me. "It's a well-known fact that blacks exploit other blacks more than anyone else exploits them. This started way back in Africa. It was the black chiefs who sold their own people into slavery – and it's a well-known fact that most black girls are molested at a very young age by their own relatives or friends of relatives. There's nothing we can do about it. It's part of their culture that they accept. They have different values from us. Their culture is sexually promiscuous. They don't buy that puritan ethic. We can't interfere in their sex lives. We just teach them economic survival."

"But isn't this a criminal case?" I asked.

"The police won't do anything about it. It'll just be your word against theirs. They'll turn it all around and make you look like the guilty party. Believe me, we've been involved in a case like this before, and we learned our lesson. We can't change their culture overnight. It'll take a few more generations before they catch up with us."

I was becoming discouraged with my work there. Their problems seemed too staggering. Who was I anyway? Was I trying to play God, as I had been accused? Nobody seemed too concerned.

Maybe I'm just too naive, not really looking at reality the way it is. After all, the director himself told me how these hard-core really are. The mayor completely ignored my letter. The head counselor was interested only in his own sexual gratification and preserving his government job. The school administrators were not too concerned about my "startling" revelations. Maybe I am just a naive, hopeless idealist.

Yet I had seen too much good in these so-called "hard-core." They had shown their true feelings in their poetry, essays, and autobiographies. In their writings they expressed their longing for a better life, for love and creativity, but the ugly reality of the streets made that dream almost impossible. The betrayal of the dream expressed itself as extreme rage, in uncontrolled violence. The young had been too disillusioned by the present world. They had been too damaged, too exploited, and they had lost hope. They had become heartsick, and many were in despair.

But hope dies slowly. The dream still slumbers under the frozen ground, waiting for the right conditions to spring forth again. People of higher consciousness must get together and create a nurturing climate where the dream can burst forth especially for our young children.

Chapter Six

THE HARDCORE SPEAK

Theresa Speaks

"Hi, my name is Theresa Sonia Thompson. I'm sixteen, black and a Scorpio. Well, my story beings on how I was raised, who raised me, and about the sad and exciting things that took place in my life.

When I was thirteen months old, I was placed in a foster home with a Mrs. Wells and her husband. They really gave me love and treated me as their own. She raised me like I should have been raised, but I was kind of hard-headed, but I did listen.

My foster father was real nice, even though we didn't see him. Often he got sick and was in and out of hospitals and rest homes. I remember the times when he was there, when Mama would get ready to spank us and we would run to my father's rocking chair where he would be sitting, and he wouldn't let her spank us. He died in 1969 of natural causes, I love him a lot and will never forget him.

I had two younger brothers named Richard and Edward. They were foster kids too. She kept them when they were babies. Richard is eleven, and Edward is about nine. We had an older brother named David. He was her real son and our big brother. He is about thirty now. Those were eleven happy years, except when my father passed away and Edward had an accident. I guess I'll tell you about it.

One day Edward was playing outside and fell down three steps. He came into the house crying. Then he started throwing up, and blood rushed from his mouth. So we put a bucket underneath his mouth and took him to Children's Hospital. When we got there, they stopped the hemorrhage and told us they would like to keep him overnight for observation.

The next morning we went to the hospital and were informed that Edward had a small hole in his throat in which a tube had been inserted so that he could breathe through it. They said he had to stay in the hospital, because he had to swallow and they would have to feed him through his veins until they were able to stretch his esophagus. He remained in the hospital about four or five months and then was released for the time being. He had to eat baby food at first, and my mother had to take him to the hospital twice a week for checkups.

About six months after he came out of the hospital, the court decided to take him from my mother, saying she was getting too old to accept the responsibility of taking him back and forth to the hospital. They were wrong. My mother never missed a turn taking him to the hospital twice a week. She really spent most of her time with my brother.

About four months later I was placed in another home because of the same thing. The court said that my mother was too old to take care of me. The home wasn't nice at all. Our foster mother didn't treat us right at all.

In three years I was placed in another home. Then four more homes followed in one year. I kept running away from those homes and kept running the streets, where I learned about dope and sex. I had to keep going to different schools all the time and hardly had time to make friends. I used to be a good student when I was with my first foster mother, but later nobody cared, and I didn't care either. I got in trouble with the police, and they put me on probation for running away.

I had to come to this school. I liked it fine, because the counselor, Mrs. Green, really cares about the girls. She understands us.

Mrs. Cummins, I'm sixteen now, and lots of girls my age have babies already. I'd like to have a baby of my own, my own flesh and blood, somebody that I could love, somebody that would love me. I don't have a boyfriend either. I guess it's because I'm kind of fat. But if I had a baby, I could get a boyfriend. All the girls that have babies get money from the county, and the dudes like a girl that's on the county.

I wouldn't give none of my money to those dudes for their dope and their booze. I'd keep the money for my baby. I'd buy it lots of nice clothes and good food. I'd take it everywhere with me. Then I wouldn't have to be without a family like right now. I've tried to get pregnant, but I can't.

What should I do, Mrs. Cummins?

Robert Speaks

I was born on February 5, 1956, to a black soldier and his Japanese wife in the hospital of Fort Ord Army installation located in Northern California. My family left for Japan when I was a little over two years old and returned two years later to Los Angeles.

My memories of life in Japan are few but happy. I remember Santa Claus emerging from a helicopter one Christmas with gifts for my friends and me. I remember parades and beautiful costumes. My mind can still conjure up the image of the Pacific Ocean at sunset from a cliff high over the water. I can still savor the taste of crabs cooked in a very special way and sold in the open market scattered along the streets of Kobe. These were some of the happiest moments in my life.

After moving back to the States, my mother and father were divorced, and my sister and I were left with relatives. Life was good…but it treated us rougher as the years passed. My sister and I spent part of 1966 and 1967 in Arkansas and then came back to California to be reunited with our father. He was retired from the Army and hoped to be able to settle down and keep us with him until we reached adulthood.

But life was cruel. I can't say exactly what happened, but my family started to fall apart. I turned to drugs and started running the streets. I became involved in the narcotics trade, gambling, prostitution, and many other forms of illegal activities.

In 1970, after being released into the custody of my father, I became involved in the "Movement" along with many other young blacks who felt the "System" was wrong. I was elected Minister of Defense at Carver Junior High School and played a large part in the protest activities that took place in the early part of the year. After being arrested and prosecuted for a felony which I didn't commit, I became bitter and again took to the streets. There I learned of the suffering of black people in America. The streets showed me how hard life is and how futile is the struggle to defeat the system without an education.

So now I've decided for the sake of future generations to get an education and try to get in position to help people. I feel now that the world must change if it is to survive, and that I am obligated to struggle – as so many before me have struggled and died to make the world a better place for mankind.

BEAUTIFUL

by Robert Sparks

Beautiful.
That's all I can say.
It's a description of you
every day...you're beautiful.

I watch you walking
and my heart starts talking
about love
And girl, I need you.

Where you going, my friend,
On this timeless day
with your feet and your face
pointing opposite ways?
Pretty soon you'll split in two,
and it'll cause the destruction of you.

Can you see the ghetto?
Can you fell the pain?
Have they yet registered
on your split-level brain?

Your turn your head and walk away.
You won't listen to what I say.
For your lack of concern you will pay
a price to me on freedom day.

You say I should be peaceful
while you beat me with sticks.
You say, "Sincerity pays," and yet you use tricks.
You say I'm free, yet my rights are denied.
So all you have done so far is lied.

Christopher Speaks

THE LIFE OF A BLACK MAN

To be black you must be proud of the word <u>black</u>, because the word <u>black</u> is a color that has been around for a very long time. But the color black is not what I am talking about. I'm talking about the race. A race that has been around for a long time, and we need to keep the black race in the running. I am proud of my race, and you should be proud of your own race also.

Today you may find one fourth of the young black men are in prison, one fourth are in gangs, one fourth are in some little business, and the other one fourth are dead. So let's talk about the one fourth that the white man is afraid of most – and that is the gangs, because the ones that are in prison cannot harm them, and the dead cannot do anything. So that leaves the living gangs.

The gangs are helping the white man by killing their own people. Every time a black person hurts another black person, that is one less person that the country has to feed. The more black people that the white man starves, the more money they can save. Everyone knows that the more money you have, the more power you have. So in order to get money, you must use your mind.

I know for a fact that not all black people are stupid as the white man thinks we are, but the ones running around the streets like a pack of dogs are doing a good job of playing stupid. It is the young black men of today who are the ones who will be running the world in the future, and if the only education that the young black man has is running around the streets like a pack of dogs, then the younger black children will learn to run the streets like puppies. So the young black man should wise up and use the mind that God gave them.

Jacky Speaks

BIOGRAPHY OF A YOUNG GIRL

This story starts way back in 1974. This young girl was only eleven years old at the time. She had stayed home from school one day. Her mother was at work, and her father was sleeping in the living room.

A few minutes later her father woke. He called her to the living room and told her to lie down beside him. The young girl thought nothing, so she lay down beside him. After a while he tried approaching her under her blouse.

She asked her father why he was trying to touch her. He then got up and went into his bedroom and called the young girl into the bedroom. He told her that she had hurt his feelings for thinking he would do such a thing. He told the girl how much he loved her.

A few weeks later the young girl's mother had been at work, and her brothers were sent off to the store. The girl had been in her room, trying to keep away. Next thing she knew, her father was trying to approach her again. Luckily, one of her aunts came over to visit, so that went by. The young girl didn't bother to tell her mother, because she was frightened.

Then a week later the young girl was in school. She received a summons from the office notifying her to come at once. As soon as she entered the office, she saw her father sitting there. The next thing she knew, she was being checked out of school because of a dentist appointment. She became terribly scared while walking out of the school. The same day was report-card day. Her father handed her the report card. She glanced at it and saw a <u>D-U-U</u> in history. At that time we used to get three swats for every <u>U</u>, five swats for every <u>D</u>. If we dared get a <u>Fail</u>, we would not be able to sit for days.

As they arrived home, her father told her she wouldn't get any swats if she did something. But she said, "No." Then he gave her about twenty swats. Then she started asking him why he was trying to hurt her, and if he didn't leave her alone, she would have to tell her mother.

All of a sudden the man blew up. He slugged the young girl and threatened to kill her. She had a bruise on her face. He told her if her mother asked where she got the bruise, to say she fell down. So the girl did so, because she was afraid of this man.

So it happened that the girl would get hit for every little thing. Her father told her she would get hit for every little dirt on the walls or around the house. He would inspect the house so good, it was pitiful. He told her it would go on until she would change her mind about things.

About a week went by. One evening when everyone was asleep, he tried doing awful things to her. She started crying and begging him to please leave her alone. So then he tried approaching her for quite a while. The girl was so scared, she didn't know what to do.

So another week later the girl's father went to her school and checked her out again. This time he took her home and raped and beat her with an electric cord, which left her with big welt marks. The marks were so bad, she couldn't even dress for gym. This only meant more beatings, because she would fail gym for nonsuits. So there went another ten swats. The girl got very hurt, so she decided to run away from home, but her father tracked her down and took her back home.

The young girl's mother went on vacation in Hawaii for a week. The girl begged to stay at an aunt's house, but they didn't let her, because she had to cook and clean house for her father and brothers. Every night that week after everyone was asleep, he would go into the girl's room and do the same thing.

The girl would pray to God that her father would stop. Every day and every night she prayed. The girl became very sad, confused, and lonely. She was so frightened, she did not know what to do. Her father would not allow any of her friends to come and visit her or even call. Besides, she was in shock and didn't talk to anyone in school.

The young girl wanted very much to tell her mother, but she was afraid her father would kill her or beat her to death. This had gone on for quite a while. The girl's mother and father got along so well, she didn't want to break up their marriage, nor their family.

A few months later the young girl was looking through her father's papers and belongings and ran across a birth certificate and other papers saying she was given away and found out her name wasn't her real name. Her birthdate had also been changed. She was born in another country. This hurt the girl very much. One day she tried to commit suicide by an overdose of pills but didn't quite make it.

In 1978 this young girl had still been going through problems with her father, getting raped and badly beat. She didn't go out with any boys, because she was afraid they would do the same thing, and she didn't want that. Finally one day the girl got so badly beaten that she had a fractured jaw, black eyes, and fractured head that required stitches. She couldn't take it anymore. She ran from the house, went to a phone booth, and called her mother.

The young girl told her mother her father had hurt her very bad. The girl was crying, telling her mother that she wanted to die, that she needed her badly, because she had been hurt. So the young girl's mother met the daughter at a certain place. The girl told her mother everything, so the mother filed a report, then called the father at a telephone booth, and had her daughter tell him that she had told her mother everything he had done to her. So the father got very upset and told the girl he was going to kill her. The young girl and her mother stayed in a hotel.

The next day the girl went to school. After school she saw her father driving around the school. The girl became very frightened and called her mother because her stepfather was after her, trying to kill her for telling her mother everything. This man always carried a handgun. This is why she was so afraid.

Then they had to move to another city, because her father was desperate to kill her, like a mad dog, asking all her friends if they had seen her because she had run away from home. He used phony lies to see if they would tell him, but no one knew where she was.

Then came June 14th, the day of court. The poor girl was afraid. She didn't want to go in there with that man. But court went on, and after court came the biggest shock.

She and her mother were in a hiding place in another city so that they wouldn't be found. The only people who knew were one uncle and one aunt. Later on that evening the young girl heard a scream. She ran downstairs to see what was wrong. She saw her aunt and uncle trying to hold her mother together. Everyone was crying. She asked what happened. They told her that her father had committed suicide. The young girl was screaming and yelling it was all her fault. If she hadn't said anything, he would still be alive.

Until this day all of the young girl's aunts and grandmother call her a whore and say it is all her fault for everything. The young girl cries very much, apologizing to everyone, telling them it wasn't her fault. She was just afraid to say anything to anyone. So the young girl couldn't stand to live at home anymore. It just brought bad memories and nightmares. She couldn't sleep.

To top it off her brothers hated her and always called her a whore and kept telling her that it was all her fault for their father's death. The girl felt very upset, thinking she broke up a family. So the girl left home, thinking she didn't belong there because she wasn't welcome. She thought things would be better for the family if she left.

The girl was away from home for quite a while, but she missed everyone. She didn't have anyone to talk to. Nine months had gone by. Finally she had built up enough courage to phone her mother to see if she could come home.

The reason the girl wanted to go back home was because she needed a family, someone to love her. She had no one. Of course, she had a boyfriend who loved her very much, but she wanted more. She needed a mother to talk to, because she never had one to talk problems over with. Then her mother said to come back home, so she did.

Weeks later the young girl's clothes were all given away. The girl became very hurt. Also, the grandmother was still calling the girl a whore and asking why she did come back. It hurt the mother to see how the grandmother was treating the girl. The grandmother kept saying that she didn't understand why her daughter had adopted the young girl.

Things that had been said to the girl hurt and changed her a great deal. So until this day this young girl is thinking of leaving again. She doesn't want to leave home, but it has to be. She's very disturbed at times. She thinks she's going crazy. She's not her real self, although she's searching for herself.

This story goes on and on inside of her.

Why can't they understand?

Is there anyone who could at least try to understand?

Jacky is an attractive young woman. She dresses stylishly and provocatively. Everyone notices her when she walks up and down the classroom with her thin high heels clicking away rhythmically. One could describe Jacky as hyperactive, unable to concentrate but quite intelligent, someone looking for attention.

For several days Jacky seemed extremely sad and depressed.

I kept asking her, "What's the matter? Why are you so depressed?"

"It's family problems. I have to leave home."

"Jacky, when will you finish your English contract? You've been working on your composition assignment for weeks. Why don't you finish up so you can get your high school credits and graduate?"

"I don't know what to write about."

Jacky was sitting in my chair at my desk. She really wanted to talk but could not.

Intuitively I replied, "Why don't you write 'A Biography of a Young Girl?'"

"That's a good idea. I'll write over the weekend, but you have to promise that you won't tell a soul about it."

"I promise, Jacky."

The following school day Jacky handed me a thirteen-page handwritten autobiography, again reminding me to keep everything in total confidence and not to read this in school but wait until I got home. She made me promise to return the writing to her so that she could destroy it herself. I swore total secrecy, thinking she wrote about the usual teenager-parent conflict or perhaps some boyfriend troubles.

I was not prepared for this shock. <u>What can I do? What is my responsibility in this case</u>?

The damage had been done long ago. Jacky was almost eighteen now. The father had been dead almost a year. She was not being sexually abused anymore, but she was suffering deeply. I saw her writing as a cry for help.

I discussed this with a school psychologist. She told me about a program called "Daughters Anonymous," and she gave me their number. This agency is comprised of trained counselors and young girls who have been sexually abused by relatives. They get together for rap sessions and express their feelings of rage, hurt, worthlessness, and guilt. They get understanding and moral support.

The next day in school, how would I react to Jacky, and how would she react to me? I decided to be natural and spontaneous. She came in and sat down. She was very quiet and would not look at me.

When everyone settled down to do their work, I returned Jacky's writing with a note: "An excellent composition. You have now completed your contract. Let's have lunch today and talk about this some more."

Jacky did not say a word. I felt that perhaps she was sorry for having written so openly. She seemed to be ashamed. She stayed in the classroom until everyone had left. I walked over to her and hugged her and gave her a kiss. We both started crying.

"You know, miss, my aunts push me away when I try to hug them or give them a kiss. They think I'm filthy, unclean. They think that I'm a whore. They still think that my father would have lived if it hadn't been for me."

"Jacky, let's go to lunch and talk about this."

"All right, miss. I don't have to go home right away after school."

In the car I started talking. "Jacky, you're a real strong girl to have experienced so much pain and yet still function and carry on a normal life. Many girls would have to be hospitalized in institutions if they'd gone through what you're experienced – but you should see a psychiatrist."

"Why? Do you think I'm crazy?"

"Of course not, Jacky. You're not crazy. It's just that such a burden has been placed on you. You need someone to help you carry it."

"I've already talked to psychiatrists and doctors. They examined me after my mother filed charges. I was all messed up inside, full of infections. The psychiatrists can't help."

"Jackie, you have to realize that you're not guilty. Your father was a very sick man. It's not your fault. He was the adult, and you were merely a child. Your family is blaming you because they feel terribly guilty for being so insensitive that such a thing could go on right under their noses and they weren't even aware of it."

"My mother doesn't blame me. She understands."

"Jacky, you said that you were adopted but that your grandmother is your real grandmother. How can that be?"

"My mother is really my aunt. My real mother was my grandmother's other daughter. My parents abandoned me and my brother when we were babies. Some neighbors found us alone and almost starved to death. So the younger sister decided to adopt her sister's two children. Nobody knows what happened to my real parents."

"Oh, so that's why your mother looks so young."

"Yes. Most people think that we're sisters. Some of the guys that I bring home fall for my mother. They think she's my oldest sister. My grandmother keeps saying that I'm just like my real mother – a whore and no good. She really hates me. She never treated me good. I had to be the maid in that house ever since I can remember. My father didn't want to take me or my brother either, but my mother insisted."

"Jacky, was your father mean to you all the time?"

"Oh, no, miss. Sometimes he was real good to me. He took me shopping and bought me all kinds of clothes and presents. Many times he was sorry after he mistreated me and took me out shopping and bought me all kinds of presents. Want to see a picture of him?"

"Sure. You have one on you?"

Jacky opened her wallet to show me two colored photographs of a very handsome young man, sensitive and artistic-looking. How could that beauty and sensitivity mask such ugliness and cruelty? Yes, I could see, there was still love for the cruel father – love, anger, hatred, and guilt.

Oh, Jacky, how will you treat a son when you have one?

I heard recently that she gave birth to a son.

Chapter Seven

HIGHLAND PARK HIGH SCHOOL

After two disappointing programs it was great to be a part of a well-functioning, effective school. Don Rogers was a strict yet compassionate principal.

Even though we were a small school, around two hundred students, we had an excellent program. Besides the usual academic high school requirements, we offered art, ceramics, wood shop, horticulture, and gardening classes. We had excellent homemaking and P.E. programs. Most classes were quite small, no more than twenty students per teacher. The principal also taught a couple of classes in horticulture and gardening.

During summer days some students were able to work outdoors under umbrellaed patio tables. Many of the students had experienced success for the first time.

Quite often a student would ask, "Why do we act so differently here? In the big high school we would be troublemakers and disturb the classes. We'd ditch a lot and not do our work. It's amazing how differently the kids act here. Why?"

My reply was usually the same. I explained to them that here they were known on an individual basis. They were not lost in the crowd. Since the classes were small, the teachers could pay them much more attention. In regular school a teacher often had one hundred eighty students per day. This did not leave much time for individual attention. Even though we wanted to help everyone, there just was not enough time in fifty-five minutes to teach a lesson, grade papers, keep the discipline, and record grades. Students were more or less on their own. They either got it or failed. Here we had time to treat them as individuals, not just as a part of a large assembly line.

Many students at Highland Park were gang members who had recently been released from juvenile hall. They were sent to continuation to make up their high school credits and return to the regular school if they wished, but most preferred to stay.

One particular student, Philip Zamora, came to my attention because many students clustered around him. He seemed to have a lot of respect and influence with many students. When I asked Mister Rogers about him, he told me that Philip was the leader of "Los Avenues," a local youth gang. As one of his English assignments, I had Philip read the poem "Gang Fight." I asked him to write an analysis of the poem. Here is what he wrote:

> This poem really makes a Chicano gang member think. The words try to express real feelings. Like "Wine" may be symbolizing confusion. "Hot" could mean anything from crazy to wild. It's really a good poem, because it deals with gang members to help them to end gang warfare. We are all brothers. But we don't see that. Do we have to cut each other up and take blood samples to find out that we are brothers? I don't think so. But this poem has to keep in mind that not always is a guy going to just stand there and let the other guy or guys cut him up until they see that this guy is not going to fight back.

There is <u>pride</u>! I don't know what to say about pride, except that pride leads to destruction. We Chicanos have pride among our Barrios. In the city there are many Barrios, all with their own pride in their neighborhood. Maybe our pride in the Barrio is strong, and we say that our pride will never lead to destruction, maybe destruction to others – but not to us. But that's not true. If we look at each other as Chicanos instead of Barrio So and So, we realize that we are really destroying ourselves. Pretty soon there won't be any more Chicanos, because we all have our "pride." If we could see how the future might be, I see it as the Barrios fighting to a last fight. I've heard people say, "Why don't you just have one big shootout with all the gangs, and just kill each other all at one time?" Well, that's just about what it's heading for. Maybe we say that it will never happen. But it already is happening. One at a time a guy from the Barrio is getting killed.

Let's think about the future and say that <u>Los Avenues</u> fight to a finish with Cypress Park, Frogtown, or all the rest of the gangs that don't get along with us. Suppose that <u>Los Avenues</u> win all the fights. We'll be bragging about being number one, and then some other gang that we do get along with will say that they're number one. What happens next, another fight for pride? Where will it all end? I don't know. Pride hides all true feelings. If nobody wants to humble themselves, then pride will go on to destruction. God help us, cause we're all scared and confused.

Will the gangs ever end all gang warfare? We could only hope for the best. I don't know why most of us do the things we do, speaking mainly of our graffiti, shootings, fighting, loitering, drinking, etc. Maybe it's because we're just so damn fed up with life, and we don't really give a shit if we live to see tomorrow, or is it the negative attitude we have in saying, "Things aren't going to get any better, just worse. One good turn leads to another." Can anyone help us now that half of our brain cells are shot from getting high when we were in our junior high school years? Most of us live in a dream world, fantasizing our power, then putting it to use in the only way we know – destruction. Destruction not only to society but to ourselves as well. Can money buy us the things we need to escape the gang world to enter reality as it really is? Do people really care enough to gamble their money on us to help end all this mess? I don't know, but I'm still hoping for the best.

I was totally amazed by Philip's deep insight into the gang problem at such a young age. He brought up some important issues and problems.

One day he also brought in his drawings. Now here was a multitalented young man, but one enmeshed deeply in a destructive lifestyle. Especially impressive was his ink drawing of a glamorously dressed skeleton representing a gang member.

"So you know, Philip, that all this gang activity is nothing but glamorized death?" I asked.

"Of course we know that now, miss," he answered matter-of-factly.

When I asked him when he joined, he told me that it was in junior high school and that he was forced into it.

At thirteen years of age, some older boy at school asked him, "Where you from?"

"From my mother," was his smart reply.

For this he received an instant bloody nose. He said he eventually had to join or form his own gang just to keep from being beat up. He also told me that the older guys – the <u>veteranos</u>, most of them in their twenties – recruited young boys into the gangs. They take them to the beach on picnics, buy them wine and beer, and befriend them. Later they give the young boys guns and ask them to commit burglaries for them, telling them that nothing will happen to them, because they are still juveniles. The older guys had already been through the juvenile system and were quite aware what young kids can get away with. Some of them had served time as adults and did not want to repeat the experience, so they asked the young boys to do the dirty work.

"What happens if you refuse?" I asked Philip.

"Well, then you're considered a chicken and a traitor, and they threaten to kill you because all traitors deserve to die."

"How can you get out then?" I wanted to know.

"There are only three ways. You either move away, get married and have a baby, or join the Army, but most of the gang members end up becoming old jailbirds. When you get out and can't find a job, because you can't do anything and have a lousy attitude, you just go back to the same old thing you know – crime."

Philip told me that most of the parents are not even aware of what their children are doing. Most do not have fathers who live at home, or the fathers work hard and are too tired, but some fathers actually encourage their sons to be in gangs, because they used to be in them also and believe it's a real macho thing to be a gang member.

One morning another student approached me, saying, "Miss, you're paying Philip so much attention because he's smart and he's an artist, but nobody needs artists these days. My uncle is even a better artist than Philip, but he couldn't get a job. He has been in prison for a long time. He has time to practice his art, but whenever he gets out, nobody needs him, so he goes right back again. Nobody gives him a job, because nobody needs artists."

Mike was one of the students with very low reading skills. His remarks did make me feel a bit guilty, because it was true that I was paying Philip a lot of attention. I told Mike that if he wanted to learn to read, I was willing to teach him; so each day while the other students were working on their assignments, I spent some time with Mike going over phonics and having him do a lot of oral reading.

We were both proud of his fast progress. He even began doing some writing. One day he handed in a paper telling how he felt when he first came to Highland Park School:

WHEN I FIRST CAME TO THIS SCHOOL.

I felt strange because it has been so long since I went to school. My friend came here, so I thought I would come here too. Then days went by, and I got used to it after a while. But now I feel I have to come just to do something. I feel like it's a place where I'm welcome, and I'm glad because it helps me out.

It always amazed me how much a little personal attention can accomplish. Are we all so wrapped up in ourselves that our children go unnoticed? Just as I was basking in our educational progress, Mike dropped a bombshell on me without any warning signs.

Out of the blue he told me quietly, "Miss, I don't want to live anymore. What should I do?"

My shocked reply was, "Mike, why are you saying such a thing? What happened?"

He told me that his girl friend was breaking up with him, that nobody loved him. Once before when he had been in love, his girl friend moved away and left him to suffer all alone. He mentioned the problems at home. His father had been drinking and beating his mother when he was drunk. Mike said that he and a brother threatened the father, that the father left the family, and that now they were having financial problems. Nothing ever worked out for him, and he did not see a way out.

We teachers are not trained psychologists, nor are we taught in any of our teaching classes how one might respond to this kind of problem. Mainly we have to rely on our own life experiences, wisdom, or lack of wisdom to cope with the unexpected.

I agreed with Mike that life is not easy, that it is a real struggle to continue living sometimes, but he had a family, people who loved him. I told him to think of his mother and grandmother. I told him suicide was the easy way out. It took real courage to face our pain and hope tomorrow would be better. Life constantly changes anyway, just like the weather. One day it rains, but the next day the sun shines.

"No, miss. Things won't change for me. If I weren't such a chicken, I would kill myself."

I told Mike that he did not kill himself because he had enough courage to live, that he was not a chicken. I asked him to write down his feelings on paper and turn them in as an English assignment. Mike told me that he would be too embarrassed to write about his feelings.

Somehow my lame encouragement that he use someone else's name worked. To my surprise, Mike handed in this paper two days later:

THE BOY WHO HAD TWO LOVERS

His name is Art Lopez. He wasn't a bad guy. All he wanted never came true. He wished that he was dead sometimes just to get away the easy way. He met a girl when he was fourteen years old. Her name was Lucy Arrona. She lives in Delano, California, and Art lives in Los Angeles. He saw her as much as he could. He would see her maybe two times a month, and that's when he was lucky. He wrote to her, and she wrote back. At first he did not believe her when she wrote him that she loved him.

Art said, "You can't love me."

She said, "But I do love you."

They still write to each other, but he doesn't see her as much as before.

Then he met someone else, and now Art is seventeen years old. He sees her every day, and her name is Norma Gomez. She loves him, and he loves her. But Art doesn't know what to do. But whatever he does, he will try not to hurt either of them. Linda hurt Art one time, but Art never forgave her, because when you are in love and you get hurt, it hurts like a mother fucker. You won't forget the pain. That's how much it hurts. Art felt like he had been shot right in his heart. Art gave his love away, and Linda had rejected it. But after a while Art forgot a little how it had hurt. Norma was a dream to him. She was what he really wanted.

Then one Friday night Norma had become a nightmare. Art would have done anything for her. But she hurt him so bad that he can never forget. He gave his love to her too. But all she wanted to do was play with his love.

Norma told him she loved him, and Art believed her. But what Art is going to do is, he won't give his love away anymore. He is tired of being in pain. But it always happens to Art. Art don't look forward to tomorrow. His heart bleeds too much, and he doesn't understand why it happens to him. Art won't try to kill himself, but he wishes he wasn't walking here on earth. Art doesn't want to get serious with anyone else after he gets away from all this.

Even though Mike was not from the same gang as Philip, they became good school friends. Philip continued to amaze me with his drawings and calligraphy.

One day I asked him, "Where did you learn those Gothic letters? With a talent like that, you could get a job as a sign painter. This way you would still be writing on buildings, but getting paid for it instead of getting in trouble."

"Then why don't you get me a job?" was his earnest reply.

I wanted to show Mike and Philip that artists are needed, that they do make money with their talent, and that people do care.

That afternoon and evening I kept trying to come up with an idea of where I might go to ask for a job for Philip. All the students really needed to see that skill and talent do pay off. I thought perhaps the local chamber of commerce would be a good place to begin.

That evening as I picked up the local newspaper, I was really surprised to see a photograph of the newly elected Chamber of Commerce president. His name was Larry Hattler, and he happened to be the owner of the local Quick Print Company. I decided to begin there.

The next morning I asked Philip to give me samples of his drawings and calligraphy, because I had an idea where he might be able to get a job.

After school I drove to Quick Print and introduced myself to Mister Hattler. After he looked at Philip's work, he told me that indeed he was looking for a layout artist. He wanted Philip to come in for an interview the next day. I could not wait to get to work the next morning to give Philip the good news.

To my great amazement and joy, Philip was hired to work there after school and on Saturdays. Mister Hattler was very pleased by Philip's work, and he became a friend of the family. I often stopped in to check on Philip's progress. All of us at Highland Park were very proud of him and pleased by his deserved success. Our students did realize that society rewards talented artists. We were all in high spirits when school closed for a week for Easter vacation.

Next Monday morning when we returned, the first sentence I heard was, "Miss Cummins, have you heard about Mike? He's in the hospital. They almost killed him. Eight guys jumped him with baseball bats. He had permanent brain damage. He was beat up so bad that his own mother didn't even recognize him. His face and hands were so swollen, his mother told the cops that wasn't her son. He might not even live."

As I listened in shock, my first thought was my conversation with Mike when he told me that he did not want to live.

My God, Mike. You said that you didn't have the guts to kill yourself. Did you find someone to do it for you?

My calm answer was, "We'll visit him in the hospital as soon as he can have visitors."

Someone suggested that we take up a collection for flowers. Philip was really angry. He wanted to find out who the cowards were who did this to Mike. It was one thing to fight man to man, but another for a whole gang to jump one person walking alone at night. He had just left Norm's house on Easter night.

Of what use was all that effort we had made to teach Mike to read? What about his mother, all the effort she had made in raising him from infancy? If he lived, he would just be like a vegetable.

Now I was really concerned about Philip. He wanted revenge. All this talk about brotherhood seemed to be forgotten.

"These cowards have to be punished before they can do more damage. I'll find out who did it. There are always squealers who do anything for a few bucks."

"Just wait until we see Mike. Maybe he can tell you something." I wanted to stall for some time, hoping that reason would eventually displace passion.

We collected enough money to be able to bring Mike a beautiful bouquet of flowers. Philip and two other students went to Glendale Aventist Hospital intensive care unit to visit Mike. When we arrived, his mother and Norma were there. Mike lay there in traction with his head and face bandaged. We talked to him and touched his arm, but we did not really know whether he was conscious or not. Philip asked him some questions privately, but on the way home he told us that Mike could not tell him anything.

We were all deeply moved by Mike's pain and frustrated by our own inability to help him. We saw the senselessness of this act, how much pain it brought not only to Mike but to his whole family. Here was another wasted young life, and for what? We needed to express our confused feelings.

On our drive back we talked about how this gang activity had to stop; how revenge, no matter how justified, leads to more death and more sorrow to a never-ending spiral of hate and destruction.

When I got home, I read some of Mike's writings and composed them into a poem. The next day I showed Philip what I wrote.

He said, "I also wrote something about Mike. I'm going to send it to Low Rider magazine."

Philip handed me the following "Open letter":

This letra is for all the Chicano gang members but is really meant for those few but proud vatos with baseball bats who all participated in the "macho" beating of El Mike de Highland Parque, the prime-time cholo who got his entire face rearranged for him at no charge on the night of Easter Sunday. Wow, I've got to admit, you so-called vato locos really did a number on him. Did you hear how he looked? His nose is completely busted. He has two black eyes, no teeth, broken cheekbones and chinbone. His whole jaw is broken. His head is split open right between the eyes, and you dudes really did a firme trabajo on his manos. He's dying of a blood clot from when you guys hit him on the neck twice with a bat, and he can't talk or use his hands to say anything.

Mike wasn't my homeboy. In fact, our barrios didn't even get along too good, but we got along pretty firme. Mike has always been a real cool dude, and he seemed to get along with everyone. I used to go to a continuation school with that dude, and he seemed like he was just beginning to enjoy life with his new ruca, Norma, who has been with him through his recent scene of misery because she cares about him. As long as I have known Mike, he was never able to throw chingasos too good, pero he was cool. Well deme you few but proud "vato locos," what the hell is your trip? You vatos just put your varrio down as well as yourselves with what you just did. That wasn't big of you, and it doesn't make you seem macho to anyone else. Is this your way of letting everyone who the so-called "Numero Uno Big Time Varrio" is? If it is, then let me tell you, you didn't prove shit. If you vatos were so "big-time," then why couldn't just one of you homeboys kick his ass instead of all of you at the same time? It's bad enough that he was outnumbered, but you guys even had to use bats on him? When it really comes down to thinking about it, you guys aren't as big as you think you are. You're a bunch of cowards, and you disgraced your own varrio by what you did. Maybe to your homeboys you're admired as vato locos, pero other varrios such as us will think of you as cowards.

This gang banging shit has got to stop! We ain't proving shit. We're just putting ourselves low by acting like animals, or in this case, cave men. I know we all have our pride, if not as an individual, then as a varrio, but what happened to "Viva La Raza?" It's long live our Chicano people, not fight to kill to be number one ganga. Gang banging only leads to the pride that brings destruction.

Why can't all of us get along and show each other up in another way that will really bring some true price in the varrio? If we want to show who's really the "big time" varrio en Los, then let's see which varrio has their shit together by competing like everyone else does in a more civilized way. Let's see which varrio will get into the "big times" moneywise. Wouldn't you feel more pride in saying, "Esa es mi varrio, todo los Chicos y Tiny Locos are high school graduates going to college to be like their admirers los veteranos who are really into the "big time" now, driving around in big cherry expensive cars, wearing expensive suits pinstriped down rando y todo, and making "big time" fedia working as lawyers, teachers, draftsmen, doctors, and all those other "big time" jalles?" That's the kind of pride I want. I want to show everyone who thinks that us gang members are no good that they're wrong. I'd rather try to get the respect of other gente by showing the pride of what I can make of myself, rather than beat the shit out of them with a bat.

If what I have just said doesn't get through your head about stopping all this gang banging, then fuck you too, and think about this. Let's say you have a boy later on. How would you feel if he got the shit beat out of him, stabbed or maybe shot to death? Think about it and remember this saying quoted from La Biblia: "Whatsoever ye desire that a man do unto you, do ye even so to them." (New Testament, Matthew 7:12) This doesn't mean to get revenge. It means whatever you want done to you, do to others. Maybe you'll jump someone again and say you never got jumped yet, cause you're so "bad," but let's see what happened with your kids. You'll probably feel the pain physically, or you'll end up feeling the pain as the parent of the guy who got his face rearranged. Either way you'll end up the loser.

I hope you won't have to learn the hard way that gang banging is dead. I did a lot of gang banging, and I had more than a dozen comrads who never even got to see their seventeenth birthday, and dozens more who got jumped, but I guess it just took this beating of El Mike to open my eyes and realize that there's no pride in being a coward. Gang banging just ain't where it's at. Don't think that I'm just talking shit either, because I'm trying my best to put my words into practice among myself, and I hope that anyone else who's still gang banging reads this and gives it some thought the next time you decide to do some banging. VIVA La Raza!

> Sincerement,
> Philip "Bosco" Zamora
> Los Avenues Calle Cyps

P.S. Forgive and Forget.

We both sat there speechless for a while.

"Maybe Mike's suffering will bring about some understanding and some changes in some gang members' hearts," I said. "Philip, you letter is absolutely inspiring. It has to be published in the local paper. May I have this? I'll take it to Ralph. He has a lot of connections with the community."

"Sure, go ahead – if you think this can do some good and knock some sense into those cowards."

A feeling of relief flooded my entire being when I realized that Philip would not pursue a course of revenge. I immediately drove to Ralph Schloming's office. At that time he was the director of the Highland Park Improvement Association. Upon reading the letter he called the publisher of Northeast Newspapers and told him that he had a very penetrating letter from a gang leader that needs to be published.

A few days later Philip's picture and letter appeared on the front page of the Northeast Newspapers. He became an overnight celebrity. The phone at Larry Hattler's Quick Print office kept ringing. Some people called in their support and approval, while others were angry and threatened to kill Philip for being a rat and a backstabber. His life was in danger. People followed him and even shot at his car. I believe the police gave him special protection.

I was beginning to wonder whether I acted too rashly and did not think of the consequences of publishing this letter. What would really have been accomplished with Mike maimed and Philip dead? I began meditating in earnest for Philip's protections.

A short while later Northeast Newspapers offered Philip a job as a graphic artist. Mister Hattler gave his blessings to Philip's promotion.

A week later Jan Klunder, from the <u>Los Angeles Times</u>, called for an interview. She spoke with Mister Hattler, Philip, and me. Philip's letter was partially reprinted in that interview. With this exposure Philip could touch more hearts of young people who might have been thinking of joining the glamorous illusion of the gang world.

Now, five years later, Philip is working for the Hearst Newspapers in Los Angeles. He is married and the father of two children. He was able to prove to himself and to the community that gang members are not stupid or more evil than other youths. He has shown that when given a positive direction or choice, young people will reach for it. Too many are now taking the wrong turns in life because of a lack of positive influence in their lives. To many, belonging to a gang is having a caring "family," friends, and excitement. They become enmeshed in a lifestyle that leaves them empty and betrayed.

If we who have more wisdom and enlightenment only sit in judgment of them, devising new ways of punishment and not reaching out our hands in guidance, then aren't we guilty of a worse crime?

Through the years, the bodies have changed: but the consciousness remains the same,

Elsa Curyk.

ISBN 1-4120-4669-6